Out of Our Hands

Out of Our Hands

Encounters with the craftsmen
and craftswomen of Hokkaido

WILLIE JONES

City *of* Words

Published in 2022 by City of Words Ltd
www.cityofwords.net

Edited by John Ryle

Cover: Red-crowned crane, Tsurui, Hokkaido, 2015 © Kazuhisa Ishikawa
Photographs in text courtesy of Northern Lights / Hisashi Urashima
Photograph on page 10 of train in snow in Hokkaido © Hiro Ino
Map of Hokkaido courtesy of Australian National University

Print and digital copies of this book may be purchased from Amazon and other online
retailers. Trade enquiries to sales@cityofwords.net

Editorial enquiries to editorial@cityofwords.net

A CIP record for this book is available from the British Library

ISBN 978-1-9160783-3-8

WILLIE JONES

Willie Jones was born in Hereford, England, in 1931. He taught at St Bees School in Cumbria from 1956 to 1959, and from 1959 to 1977 at Shrewsbury School in Shropshire. From 1979 to 1995 he was a Lecturer in English at Hokkaido University, and from 2000 to 2007 Professor of English Rhetoric at Sapporo University. His essays on language and the arts of rhetoric can be found at https://ci.nii.ac.jp/en. He is also the author of works in verse and memoirs of his childhood in England and later life in Japan. He lives in Sapporo.

Contents

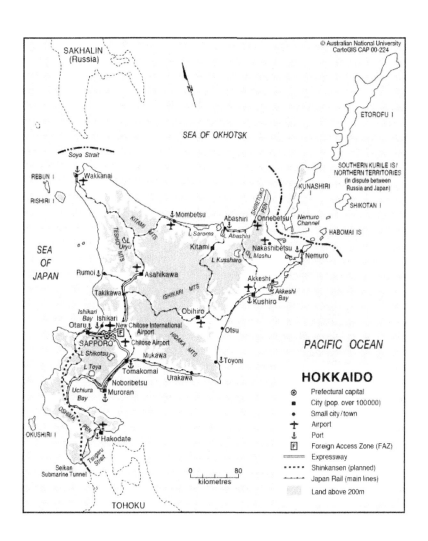

Introduction

One Sunday morning in February, 1981, I was in my office in Sapporo, on the third floor of the building that houses the Department of General Studies at Hokkaido University, putting together papers for a talk that I was due to give the next day in Obihiro, a town in central Hokkaido that in those days was five hours away by train across the mountains. Since snow in these parts falls from November to March, it already lay several feet deep on the flat roofs of buildings nearby, and after two winters of living with it every day I had grown accustomed to it. Yet I had not lived in Sapporo long enough to have appreciated that within the earth's unstable crust the tectonic plates that grip the island like the claws of a vice may grow restive. When the air quivered and the papers on my desk started to shiver I at first paid no attention. Then the desk itself began to move under my hands; bookcases shrugged their shoulders; and water in a tray on the radiator flew madly across the room. A free-standing bookcase began to tilt towards me; I leapt up and leant against it. I had taken for granted that so substantial a building was rooted, unshakeable; now I could feel its four-square, four-storey steel frame twist first one way, then another. At length, though, the shaking slowed down until, finally, girder by girder, rivet by rivet, the building settled to itself again.

I was to meet a colleague at Sapporo station, and the train was scheduled to depart at noon. I mopped up the water on the office floor, put my papers in my bag, and set off. As I descended the stairs, I noticed a crack zig-zagging down the staircase wall. At the station, we waited for news, but by five o'clock nothing had been said about when or if trains would be running again. My companion phoned a colleague who lived in Takikawa, a town a little way up the line, and we took a taxi to meet him there. Just as we arrived at Takikawa station, however, the train that we might have caught had we waited raced through without stopping, so our colleague then drove us to a station further up the line. From here we shared a carriage with an amiable if over-demonstrative drunkard, as the train carried us up and around the back of the island's mountain core. We would have been benighted at a ski resort there, had we not found another taxi that carried us in the early hours down to the broad Tokachi plain, the headlights picking out banks of deep snow on our right, with a well of darkness on our left. Not until we arrived in Obihiro did my companion dare to open his eyes. We slept on our host's living room floor.

The next morning we gave our talks to an audience of high school teachers of English, amongst them Mr Hisashi Urashima, the bright-eyed, boyish founder and principal of a local language school, English House Joy. Mr Urashima was also the publisher and editor of Northern Lights, an annual magazine in English designed to advertise and celebrate the diversity of life in Hokkaido, described on the masthead of the magazine as "the land of the pioneers", the *tonden-hei*, the soldier pioneers who were sent by the Meiji government in the late nineteenth century to colonise what was regarded as unclaimed land, though in fact it was the home of the Ainu, the people indigenous to the island. After the talk Mr Urashima approached me and introduced himself, and I mentioned that I had bought, in a Sapporo coffee shop, some pots made by a Mr Sakata, who lived, I had heard, in Obihiro. It turned out that Mr Urashima was a friend of Mr Sakata; there and then he gave me a piece of paper and a pencil and asked me to write my impression of Sakata's work for the next issue of his magazine.

The piece that I wrote appeared in Northern Lights the following July. (The essay that appears in this book was written later, by which time I had come to know Mr Sakata as well as his pots.) After that, and for the next dozen years, the magazine published articles about craftsmen and craftswomen living in Hokkaido that Mr Urashima commissioned from me. The final number of Northern Lights gathered seven of these essays together with colour photographs to form a collection that might be called a florilegium, and is now a rarity.

The expeditions that we took to meet these gifted men and women carried us from the island's conurbations to its hinterlands; it was in this way I began to understand the genius of the place that had inspired them – workers in clay and glass, wood and wool, steel and ink – votaries of what one, a glass-worker, referred to as "arrested fire", and another as "awakened stone". This book is a record of our conversations, along with reflections on the natural world and the landscapes of Hokkaido, and on those crafts that we may also call arts.

Back in 1993, when I first put the essays together, I had them privately printed under the title "Out of Men's Hands", a title to which a number of my women friends rightly took exception, not least because several of the hands were women's. For that collection I took Mussorgsky's orchestral suite, *Pictures at an Exhibition*, as my model, and my first idea had been to call the collected essays "Pictures of Some Expeditions", with an introductory preamble to set the tone, and with promenades between each of the encounters, which were conceived of as pausing in front of a picture in order to absorb as much of it as is possible in the time available. I adhered to this structure even after I had abandoned the title as being too contrived. In the present redaction the promenades have been absorbed into the visits themselves, but the underlying structure remains in place. Should any reader find the Mussorgsky framework congenial, it might still be helpful.

The title *Out of Our Hands* is intended to mean two things at the same time, meanings distinct yet related. The works that I describe in these pages are in the first place the works of men's and women's hands: several of the makers whose work I discuss – though not all of them – said that they felt a unique and unbreakable bond between themselves and what they had made, a bond that time would never breach. Nevertheless, once such works have passed out of their workshops and into the hands of someone else, they are out of the maker's hands in the sense that the maker is no longer in a position to affect or control what happens to them, and what other people do with them, or understand them. And so it may come about that over time the works of our hands acquire a certain pathos: in Latin, *lacrimae rerum*, the tears of things; in Japanese, *mono no aware*, the poignancy of things. This is the loneliness of objects that were in the past treated with love and care, but now, found on the shelves of second-hand shops, assume a condition of anonymity. Such objects carry the sign of the loneliness called *sabishi*, a state that with their love of togetherness the Japanese cannot bear, and seek at all costs to avoid. It may move us to tears.

Soon after my first visit to Obihiro in 1991, Japan Rail built a new line through an afforested bowl high in the hills that in Wales would be called a *cwm* and is now a skier's Valhalla, the monstrous Tomamu Towers. Today the trip from Sapporo to Obihiro takes little more than three hours. It is a journey I have taken on many occasions. Once the train has climbed over the island's lower back, it zig-zags down through woods before crossing watercourses shaded by native oaks and alders that parcel out rough pastures, grazed by black and white Holstein cows. The soil is volcanic ash; the Dutch-style farm buildings are red with blue skull caps; farmyards are fringed with borders of ground phlox and hedges of azalea or rhododendron. Double ranks of silver birch and larch break the cold winds that come down off the high mountains to the north. These foothills, softened to a dusky pink in a late evening sun, have a familiar feel for those with roots in Europe: they remind me of an April evening in Tuscany, while my sister, on a visit to Hokkaido, was put in mind of the partly-wooded valleys of mid-Wales, near where we grew up. Conversely, when I showed a book of photographs of the Welsh Border to Japanese friends in Sapporo, they all said that many of the landscapes reminded them of parts of Hokkaido.

Once past Obihiro the railway line carries on to the port of Kushiro, passing on its way just south of the marshes where the red-crowned cranes gather in winter. Those who study birds travel from all over the world with high-powered cameras to photograph the cranes' connubial *pas de deux*. When, over the following years, I travelled to Obihiro by myself, Mr Urashima would meet me at the station and drive me to a hotel at Tokachigawa Onsen, a hot spring resort on the northern bank of the Tokachi river. Here, if I stayed for a day or two, I would have time to walk beside the river, with only birds for company. There were herons and kites, golden-eye ducks and ringed plovers, while invisible warblers sang in the reeds. When I had the day to myself, I would walk up a wooded ridge to the north for a sight of jays, tits and finches. At a viewing spot on the way up, a bronze panorama on a sturdy wooden frame tells you what you are looking at: you can trace the course of the Tokachi River flowing off to the south-east; to the west lies the low profile of Obihiro town; beyond it rises the high, serrated profile of the Hidaka range, the tail of the island's spine that runs down to its southern tip, Cape Erimo. This was where many of the expeditions described in this book began. If we were due to meet one of the craftsmen who lived not too far away, Mr Urashima would call for me after breakfast, then off we would go.

Acknowledgments

I shall be forever grateful to Mr Urashima for giving me so rare an opportunity. There are others, too, whom I should thank. When, two years before, I had first arrived in Japan to take up my post at Hokkaido University, two of my new colleagues – Professor Nobukatsu Takahashi and Professor Hiroshi Watanabe – were waiting at Chitose, Sapporo's airport, to meet me. Nobu was a folklorist who translated German and English tales into Japanese, and Japanese and Ainu tales into English; he also translated the stories of Kenji Miyazawa, stories that Kunio Sato, one of the craftsmen I was later to meet, would one day illustrate. Nobu was my companion on that first trip to Obihiro. Had he not suggested that I should be invited to give a talk alongside his, I might never have met Mr Urashima or the craftsmen and women he would take me to meet. Nobu was a man much loved, not least by his foreign colleagues, to whom he was generous far beyond the call of duty, and when he died of cancer in his middle-fifties, we knew that we had lost a very dear friend. Professor Watanabe, the colleague who came to our rescue with his car on that trip to Obihiro is a translator into Japanese of English fiction of the eighteenth century, and a man known for his wit and his ability to play with words, not only in Japanese. Later he kindly translated some of the poems of Norio Tokita, the farmer-poet, into English for me. I had other companions on several of these expeditions: Mrs Yasuko Suginome and Mrs Shizuko Shimizu, who accompanied me on trips to meet, respectively, Prabakhar Naik Satam and Kunio Sato; and the late Keisuke Kurata, who took me to visit the Kida Museum at Iwanai.

This new version of the essays, *Out of Our Hands*, has been edited by John Ryle. My thanks to him, and to Nicholas Rankin, Roger Jones, Eri Hotta and David Campbell for their advice on various drafts, and Kazuhisa Ishikawa, for the use on the cover of his photograph of red-crowned cranes at Tsurui.

In the years since I wrote the first versions of the essays the artists and craftsmen that I met—those who are still living—have remained true to their calling. Norio Tokita has gained further national recognition for his tanka. The potter Masayoshi Sakata still lives and works in Obihoro. Yuriko Oido, the etcher, spent ten years in Malaysia, but is now back living in Japan; she held exhibitions recently in Tokyo and Sapporo. Chiyoji Asahara continues to run his glass studio in Otaru, where I visited him all those years ago, and Prabhakar Naik Satam has published a memoir of his life as a tapestry maker, called *Life After Dark*. Since 1994 Hisako Sumi (www.north-indigo.com) has been director of Earth Network (www.earthnetwork.info), an organisation dedicated to the preservation of the dye-producing flora and fauna and natural fibers that she uses in her weaving. In 2019 the glassmaker Makoto Shimazaki held a one-man show at Kushiro Art Museum in Hokkaido. Kunio Sato, meanwhile, has published many books of his wood engravings; in 2018 there was an exhibition of them in New York. He has also become an expert on the artefacts of the Jomon period in Hokkaido (http://www.yamane-kokoubou.com). The weaver Aya Kiuchi died in 2006, and in 2017 her workshop and museum were forced to close; but the citizens of Asahikawa have petitioned the city government to reopen them. Hiroshi Doi, the painter of horses, died in 1997. The fate of Toshiharo Kinoshita, the swordsmith, and that of Ryudo Nagao, the wood-carver, I have been unable to determine.

Masayoshi Sakata, potter

Since Masayoshi Sakata lived in Obihiro, we did not have far to go to meet him. It was the first of several visits I was to make to his home. A small house of greyish, snow-weathered stucco, the woodwork interiors untreated, it had been built soon after the war. Far better houses than his are frequently pulled down and whatever the owners can afford erected in their place, but Mr Sakata seemed content as things were. The traditional farmhouses of Japan, whose roof beams are tree trunks, have lasted for centuries, as they were meant to do; Mr Sakata's pots, too, are made to last, as pots always have been. Some of them are like baby pumpkins, some spherical and larger; some have long throats rising from bodies like bulbs; some have slender feet; the colours are ochre, brown or grey, sometimes black, the texture rough, while thick glazes may run in rivulets down their flanks. (I am able to describe them so precisely because I have some here beside me in my room.)

The two ground-floor rooms in Mr Sakata's house were his workshop; the upstairs room was his showroom, where he spread his futon and sat on the floor to read. Here, on low shelves, he displayed his pots. The workshop was cluttered and undusted, the large worktable stained with rings left by coffee cups and scarred by the burnt ends of cigarette stubs. The only tools that I could see were whatever scrap of metal or wood happened to be within reach, a length of wire, a kitchen knife with a broken, rusted blade. It all looked terribly ramshackle, but Mr Sakata clearly knew just where everything was.

Since much of the soil of Hokkaido is friable volcanic ash, he gets the clay he needs from Aomori, the most northerly prefecture of the main island, Honshu. When he is ready, as I saw for myself, he takes an armful of treated clay from one of the sacks piled up against the wall, hugs it to his chest and begins to wrestle with it as if it were the body of some small, recalcitrant animal. He is quite a small man – a child-sized Laocoön – but he and the clay are not angry antagonists, they are loving accomplices. He first moulds the coils into the shape of cockle-shells or chrysanthemums, and when he is satisfied, throws them onto his wheel with a satisfying thump. It is a hand-wheel, which he turns with his left hand while with his right he begins to draw out a pot; when the wheel is spinning at the correct speed, he uses both hands, pushing the clay outwards, upwards, pulling it away from the centre, all the while thinning it and shaping it, the operations under control as one hand passes the pot on to the other, as if the hands were dancing together. Homer compared this action to the movement of the young men and women dancing, hand-over-hand, with each other on the shield that Hephaestus, the Greek god of volcanic fire, made for Achilles at the end of Homer's Iliad.

Mr Sakata was inspired by a man he was too young to have met, Shoji Hamada, who revived the ancient craft of pottery in Japan. It was an aspect of Japan's cultural heritage interrupted by the country's defeat in the Second World War. If the ancient crafts are once again treasured and revered in Japan, men like Hamada are among those who deserve the credit. Mr Sakata has modelled his manner of working, as well as the kinds of pot that he produces, on the work of Hamada, on its air of spontaneity, of an easy, casual grace, of an apparent playfulness that is, in Dryden's phrase, "art hid with art", where creative mysteries are veiled by a mask of debonair unconcern.

After meeting Mr Sakata and realising what writing for Mr Urashima's magazine entailed I turned to Susan Peterson's book *Shoji Hamada: A potter's way and work*. I learned that Hamada worked for a time with the Cornish potter Bernard Leach. He returned to Japan in 1924, but they remained in touch. Leach said of Hamada that he was unable to recall "any irritation or anger between us in half a century.... Of all the men I have ever known, nobody had such a balance of heart, head and hand as Hamada." This balance of heart, head and hand as something that I was to find in all the craftsmen and women that I would go on to meet in Hokkaido. Although I may not always draw attention to it, it will be clear how essential such a balance has to be.

Keats said that poetry had better come like leaves to a tree or not at all, but he was well aware that trees need to be fed and watered, and that his own sources of nourishment were other English poets, notably Shakespeare and Milton. Likewise, when Shoji Hamada famously said that making a pot should be like walking downhill on a pleasant afternoon, he knew that we must climb to the top of the mountain before we can relax on the descent, and that this can sometimes be tougher on the thighs than when climbing it, that we need strong boots to take us to the top and should watch where we put our feet. Poets no less than potters, actors no less than athletes, can only forget themselves when they have perfected their fundamental skills.

After he returned to Japan, Hamada settled in Masiko, a village of potters in Tochigo Prefecture, but as no one had heard of him, the villagers regarded him with suspicion. Since his work did not conform to the styles for which the village was known, his revival of the more demanding traditional methods that he had learned from Bernard Leach was seen as evidence of dangerous wilfulness, and he was branded with the stigma of individualism. Although he could easily have settled in one of the great metropolitan centres, he had chosen to work in such an out-of-the-way place precisely to escape the temptations of individualism, and so avoid the sins of self-glorification, superficiality and commercialisation. Despite this initial antagonism, and without self-promotion on his part, his fame spread, until all who care about such things came to know of him and admire him as a master potter.

Such universal renown has not come to Masayoshi Sakata, nor is ever likely to, for while Shoji Hamada was open and gregarious, Sakata is a man who prefers privacy. Nevertheless, he lives in the right place, the back of beyond, and works with quiet, self-forgetful dedication. I doubt if the question of fame bothers him, and were I to ask him, he might not be able to tell me. As only the wealthiest potters have their own kilns, Sakata had to share one with a number of fellow potters, and one day, when he was driving me around Tokachi in his dusty pick-up, he took me to see it. It was a white, barrel-roofed military style hut, set down by itself at the edge of a field. Potters know that kilns fired by electricity are no match for furnaces stoked with wood, and the lengths of timber that were stacked up against the hut's outer wall had been logged nearby, in the woods that covered the hillsides like a fleece, as A.E. Housman, in his poem "On Wenlock Edge", described the forest that covers the Wrekin, a barrow-like hill in south-east in Shropshire. Since potters usually fire their pots only twice a year, the passing guest is unlikely to be present at a firing session. On the day that Sakata took me to see it, the kiln was cold; later, he gave me a photograph of himself at the open door of the kiln, white-coated like a laboratory technician, his unglazed pots on shelves at his back. He had a dream, he said, that one day he would be able to move out into the wilderness, to live next door to his own kiln, like an old charcoal burner in the woods. Mr Urashima tells me that Mr Sakata now lives near him in Obihiro, so it seems that this is a dream that he will probably have had to give up.

When I sent a photograph of my Sakata pots to a friend at the school where I had worked in England, a colleague there asked her, "What does he use them for?" I might have answered that what I do is look at them: I hold them in my hands, not only to dust them, but to remind me of their maker. While potters may know what goes into a furnace, they do not know what will come out: unforeseen faults are exposed, unlooked-for beauties disclosed: a potter's furnace is a crucible in which clay undergoes its metamorphosis, not unlike the human mind, which may be surprised by the thoughts and ideas that emerge out of the discrete experiences that it has assembled so haphazardly. Pots are among the most informative of human artefacts and the most lasting: they can tell us who lived where and when, as far down as we can dig, but they cannot tell us the names of the individuals who made them, the anonymous historians of the culture in which they lived.

Although the potters of the early Jomon culture of Japan would have made their pots for practical purposes, to hold water or rice, they also felt a need to incise on their surfaces a pattern of marks, at first only simple chevrons, but evidence of a desire to turn craft into something that we might now call art. Until recently, Japanese historians believed that Jomon culture had never reached Hokkaido, but one summer my friend Nobu invited me to go with him to Minami-Kayabe, a fishing village on the heel of Hokkaido's boot, where a friend of his student years, an archaeologist from Hokkaido University, was excavating a remote site. The pieces of Jomon pottery that the archaeologist had found confirmed his belief that early Jomon culture had once reached Hokkaido, the homeland of the Ainu; the discovery has changed how scholars now perceive the Ainu and their culture.

When the potters of ancient Greece discovered the means to do so, they painted on their pots scenes of revelry. In "Ode on a Grecian Urn" John Keats describes how such a scene teased him "out of thought"; two centuries earlier, Sir Thomas Browne, contemplating burial urns discovered during excavations in Norfolk, was moved to write *Hydriotaphia, Urn Burial*, a book about time. It is a book that I came across by chance: for all of us, a chance meeting with a work of art in any medium may affect how we think about all other forms of creative making.

Long ago in London, visiting Kenwood House, I came face to face with one of Rembrandt's most celebrated self-portraits. The painting confronts the viewer with an image of the workings of time, shown in the face of an old man in pain. It is a picture that, once seen, is never to be forgotten, though I am older now than Rembrandt was when he painted it. Similarly in Sapporo, many years later, when Japan was rich – before the bubble burst – and art exhibitions regularly toured the country, I had another experience of illumination, in an exhibition of paintings on loan from the Boston Museum of Fine Arts. It was a splendid show, with portraits by Velázquez and Cézanne, and landscapes and cityscapes by Pissarro and Monet, but the work that brought me to a halt was a painting of a teapot, set off by two bunches of grapes, three chestnuts and a pear, painted in or around 1764 by Jean-Siméon Chardin. How, I wondered, could an ordinary teapot, and a painted teapot at that, have such presence?

The answer is surely that Chardin respected the pot as having its own identity. In love with paint, he forgot himself as he worked, so that by a strange metamorphosis, the painter, the paint and the pot became one. We might see this as a rebuttal of Plato's claim that representations are twice removed from the reality of ideal forms. Not only doesa painting such as Chardin's teapot have a presence in itself, they seem to embody the essence of what it is to be a teapot. The encyclopaedist Denis Diderot, Chardin's contemporary, looking at the same paintings, was no more able than we are to understand how this could be so; he could not see, he wrote, how "the air seems to circulate around these objects." "This magic," he added, "defies understanding." In *Chardin* (1986), Philip Conisbee quotes Diderot's account of the effect that a Chardin painting, "A Jar of Olives", had upon his fellow painter Jean-Baptiste Greuze: "I have been told," wrote Diderot, "that Greuze... looked at it, and went on, heaving a deep sigh. That praise is briefer and better than mine".

No one really knows how Chardin painted a teapot or a jar of olives. And no one, I would discover later, knows how the sword-masters of old Japan created their swords. We may ask another question of works such as these, a question to which all the essays in this book address themselves, albeit obliquely. If both the painting and the pot are made with respect for the materials out of which they are made, and if Sakata's pots no less than Chardin's paintings have been fashioned with the same deep, self-forgetful love of the material out of which they are made, by what criteria are we to value the one more highly than the other? I ask this not to glorify an obscure potter on an obscure island not quite attached to the main island of Japan, but to set him in the context of the craft of making, of that side of man's nature that would create with love rather than destroy, that would praise and celebrate rather than castigate or condemn. When such works pass from the maker's hands to ours, we are caretakers for a while, and must respect the skill and the love that have gone into their making, Mr Sakata's works no less than another's. Should we attempt to possess or control that work, we may destroy it.

The craft of the potter, like most crafts, is a mystery, in the sense of being a specialised skill known only to initiates, and also in the sense of being something that not even initiates may be able to explain. Sakata himself does not really know what happens to his pots once they are inside the kiln, or why they come out as they do. While a chemist will be able to tell us what changes to the elements and compounds will have taken place, even the chemist is unlikely to be able to explain why one pot is never quite the same as another, when the process has been the same.

Swordsmiths and glassblowers use fire too, but they use it to shape the pieces that they hold in their hands; a potter must leave it to the fire to do what it will with the work that his hands have shaped. The fire that tests the potter's work may transform it into a piece that the potter never imagined: even its faults may satisfy our sense of the imperfections of all human effort and our need to accept troubles with detachment and calmness of mind. We can compare such a spirit to that of the Japanese tea ceremony, where tea bowls are passed from hand to hand and are studied with reverent care, as selected manifestations of the concepts of *wabi* and *sabi*, the acceptance of transience and imperfection.

Fire is the heart of the mystery. The Indian god Shiva, who dances the world into being, also represents refining fire, wreaking destruction in order to recreate what he has destroyed. In the tales of ancient Greece, Prometheus steals fire from the gods and gives it to man. The stories of Shiva and Prometheus are myths, of course, but when it comes to the origin of fire, myths may be all that we have.

Fire, in turn, provides imagery for human energies. Shakespeare's Berowne, in *Love's Labours Lost*, takes "the right Promethean fire" as a metonymy for man's creative power, the forge as an image of the mind. Shakespeare was fond of this image of the human brain as a kiln, or a smithy: into the kiln that is the mind goes all that the human being sees and hears. What the mind does with what it takes in may not be fully explicable, even to the neurobiologist. Our ancestors seem to have known from very early in the long process through which they became human beings how to make pots to hold things, as well as how to make tools with a sharp edge to cut, or to kill. How did they learn this?

Hokkaido is an island where earthquakes are regular events. Sudden fire is a familiar sight; volcanic eruptions still drive residents from their homes. In 2018, while I was working once again on these essays, an earthquake blacked out the whole island, in some places for days. It shifted hillsides from their roots, and buried households in their sleep. Sakata's pots reflect this reality: some are as black as basalt, some grey as steel; some have thick smears of glaze running down their sides; some look like a house that burned down in the night, blackened and blistered rafters all that are left. In the north-western parts of the Tokachi Plain where Sakata lives, hills thrust themselves upward in alpine ridges, young in geological time. The hills are ribbed with snow even in June, and often plumed with smoke from fissures in their folds or holes in the crowns of their hats. Lava sometimes flows from them, as the glazes spill down the sides of a Sakata pot. Some knowledge is as old as the hills, and it is very likely from the hills that we learned it.

Toshiharu Kinoshita, swordsmith

A party of international soil scientists I once travelled with on a field trip found it hard to believe that the volcanic ash of the Tokachi plain should be so richly farmed when hardly a hundred years had passed since the Meiji government dispatched the *tonden-hei* – the intrepid soldier-farmers – to fell the forests and till the fields. The soil scientists spoke of the newly farmed land as having been "reclaimed". It was an odd word to use to describe the transformation of virgin land into an agricultural commodity – as if the land had belonged to humans in the first place. In effect "reclaim the land" meant to steal it from the Ainu, the indigenous people who lived beside the rivers or on the shores of the lakes. The forests of Hokkaido, today as well as yesterday, are inhabited by deer and by bears, creatures with which the Ainu still live in a religious harmony. The Ainu had too much respect for the land and its non-human inhabitants to make any claim to own it.

Shortly after I met Mr Urashima for the first time he invited me back to Obihiro to give a talk at his school. So I returned to the Tokachi Plain, staying at the Tokachigawa hot springs, taking a room in what had been the first hotel there, an ancient *onsen* with a bath that I shared, on this occasion, with some workmen keen to make my acquaintance. That winter afternoon, as the vapour rising from the bath misted the broad windows, the sun going down beyond the serrations of the dark Hidaka range took on the muted tones of a Monet sunset over the Thames. Shelves of snow-weighted ice fringed the river's willow-fenced banks, while gentle plumes of steam broke through fissures in the riverine snow. After sunset, when the snowy fields turned grey, the river worked its way like a ribbon of white silk between the banks. In places the water was ruffled with the gleam of polished steel. Since those early days, a suspension bridge has been built to attract visitors to a number of new hotels, and though it has driven away the warblers and may discourage the swans, it has not bothered the black kites. Then and now they spread the tips of their feathers, showing off their dark-brown and russet underbodies as they adjust to the currents of air.

The morning after my talk at Mr Urashima's school, he rang Obihiro railway station and learned that all the seats on the train that I was planning to take back to Sapporo had been booked; this setback gave him another idea. He was driving a young American visitor, Mary Battaia, to Obihiro airport to catch a plane to Tokyo, and he decided to take me as well. He had arranged that on the way to the airport they would pay a visit to a local craftsman he was keen that she should meet; now it occurred to him that the same craftsman might also be a subject for what would be my first interview for his magazine.

Although I knew nothing of the craft in question, such a trifle would not have bothered Mr Urashima, and so, attended by the favour that was to bless us on this and on all our subsequent adventures, off we went, leaving the swans on the river whooping and blindingly white in the sun of a frosty March morning, to visit Toshiharu Kinoshita, a swordsmith.

Ten-foot high poles lined the country roads to show drivers the location of the verge beneath the snow. Though by then it had gone from the roads, the snow still lay over the wide fields like lace, glazed by a bright sun with crystalline frost. Later, Mr Kinoshita was to teach us that a sword glitters because it, too, is made of crystals. He told us that he had learned the secrets of his esoteric craft from a master-smith in Gifu Prefecture and returned to his native Hokkaido only a year or two before we met him to set up as an independent maker of swords. But it was not easy to see how he could make a living at it. In Japan, only those with a rarely-granted licence are allowed to purchase and keep swords, and such collectors are unlikely to buy a modern sword from an only recently qualified and perfectly unknown swordsmith. We had been warned that Mr Kinoshita might not at the moment have any work on hand to show us, and that he might not anyway wish to show us things that had not been finished to his liking. Since it is an ancient tradition for smiths to be secretive, their trade in every sense a mystery, we were duly apprehensive when we stopped at his tiny, newly-built house, just off the road, bounded on all sides by the snowy fields.

When Mr Kinoshita opened the door, he looked even more apprehensive than we were ourselves. But he was expecting us, and we followed him up a narrow staircase to his small tatami room, where bookcases of compressed cardboard and a paper-thin veneer leant against the walls. A low table with a sloping lead sink and a number of grinding stones stood in the middle of the room; a full tub of water stood beside it. We knelt in a small, tight semi-circle on one side of the table, while he knelt at a little distance facing us. He was a solidly-built young man, with heavy thighs and thick, crab-shaped, burn-scored hands. When he spoke he hung his head like a child who has been scolded: whether this was a sign of an elected isolation, a condition of his craft, or whether it was a symptom of *sabishi*, that unwanted and painful loneliness, I could not tell. If I had had any idea of what to ask, I might have hazarded a question, but I was feeling as diffident as Mr Kinoshita looked, and I felt that any question might have been impertinent. So I never learned why he had wanted to be a swordsmith, or what daemon had driven him to take up the craft. I remained as much in the dark about this as the peasants who used to watch at a safe distance the glow of a swordsmith's window against the blackness of the night.

This was something that I did learn, although only later. When swordsmiths forge their lengths of steel they do it in the dark: they work only by the light of the red-hot metal and the light of the furnace. And since the forge is always sited a little distance from the house, the neighbours, seeing that gleam in the night in past times, may well have felt awe, have felt that this was no ordinary craft, that there was something semi-divine about those who practised it. We know that the secrets of smiths are metallurgical rather than metaphysical, and metallurgists can doubtless explain how half-molten metal when beaten may become a sword, but the blades that the smiths forged in the smithies of ancient Japan are superior to any sword that today's smiths can produce, and nobody knows why. It is possible that magic came into it somewhere.

Since I am using the word "mystery" to characterise the work of the Hokkaido craftsmen and craftswomen who so generously invited me into their workshops – and often their homes – I should explain what I mean by it. We learn from etymologists that the English word "mystery" is derived from the ancient

Greek *myein*, "with closed eyes and lips", and in the European middle ages it came to mean the unique trade secrets of whatever particular craft you practised, for if you wished to keep your share of the market, you needed to keep your mouth shut. The arts that a craftsman practised belonged to Hermes Trismegistus, a Greek hierophant of legend, probably best known today for having been the supposed inventor of a magic sealing agent, so that we still say that something no one can open or get into is "hermetically sealed". The master of a craft guarded his secrets with a jealous eye and kept a tight seal on his lips.

I would learn after getting home that the great period of Japanese sword-making was the Kamakura Era (1185-1333). At this time swordsmiths were *yamabushi*, samurai of the mountains, their lives correspondingly austere. Money was not an issue for them, so it was said, nor was comfort; what mattered was constancy and courage, and the sword itself, *nihonto*. If a sword-maker's motives were not pecuniary, he may still have intended the uninitiated to think that he was divinely inspired, thereby acquiring power and authority; he may himself have believed that he had been specially chosen. When, around 1400, the golden age of Japanese sword-making came to an end, the quantity of swords produced rose sharply, while their quality correspondingly fell. The sword-makers of today cannot produce steel of the same quality, and metallurgists have been unable to discover why not: the secret has been lost.

In the late sixteenth century – by which time one infers that almost every man must have owned a sword – the warlord Hideyoshi promulgated a "sword hunt" to confiscate them. During the following three hundred years of the Edo era – the last feudal government, sometimes known as the Shogunate – a little of the old knowledge was recovered, but craftsmanship was diverted to the trappings: the handguard, the scabbards, the lanyards, all beautifully made and lavishly decorated. It became the prerogative of the samurai, the knightly class, to carry a sword, and the sword became a blazon, the sign that signified who you were. It was a signifier that everybody recognised, and feared. The creed of *bushido*, the traditional way of the warrior, held as its first principle that a samurai's sword must be dearer to him than a wife, though as samurai were not meant to have wives this should not have been difficult. If you were a good samurai – which not all of them were – you might never be asked to wield it, for though a samurai ought never to be afraid to use his sword, he was expected to use it only as a last resort, with responsibility and circumspection. This was the samurai creed, the way of knightly conduct. A samurai was supposed to be the servant of his sword as much as its master; and to use his sword well he had first of all to be master of himself.

I learned all this later, and as we sat in Mr Kinoshita's room in somewhat uncompanionable silence, I had no notion of what it was permissible to ask. I was sure that we would not be taken to see his forge, nor would we be told what the swordsmith did when he was there, though I learned later that the heated metal is folded and enfolded a hundred times, and that afterwards the blade is polished with a sequence of finer and finer stones. Although Mr Kinoshita's forge was out of bounds, the grinding stones were there in the room with us, and he told us that he did everything himself, leaving only the making of the wooden scabbards to others.

That might have been as much as we would have learned, had not Mr Urashima explained to Mr Kinoshita why he wished to introduce him to Mary Battaia, our American visitor. She explained that she worked in New York with a man who restored ancient pistols, and she now showed Mr Kinoshita photographs of some of these. When he realised that at least one of his visitors had more than a passing interest in his work, he stood up and went to a bookshelf for volumes of photographs of pistols, and the two experts began to compare the workmanship. For the first time since we set off, we began to relax, and Mr Kinoshita stood up again. This time he went to a cupboard and came back with two rolls of stiff brown paper. He knelt, still facing us, but now our roles had subtly changed: he was the hierophant, we the disciples. He drew off the brown paper sheaths to reveal two partly finished blades; both had been forged, but he had work still to do on the grinding and the polishing; he pointed to the different degrees of finish, and then offered the swords to us to hold. Ms Battaia took one, with, I felt, a certain hesitation. I declined. I did not believe that I had the right. And I felt a flicker of atavistic fear.

Who first had the idea of folding red-hot iron, and discovered that when the red-hot iron is mixed with burning charcoal the result will be carbonised steel? Was it because they lived next door to a volcano? Was Hephaestus their master, god both of blacksmiths and volcanoes? In Europe the first to forge iron with charcoal were the Vikings. It was around the same time that the Japanese began to forge their first *nihonto*. The Vikings traced their knowledge to Wayland the Smith, a legendary figure in Germanic mythology; for the Japanese it came by way of Korea from China. In all these cultures swords have had a symbolic role: for killing dragons or dubbing knights, for cutting off the heads of unfaithful queens, dividing a cloak, or driving Adam and Eve from the Garden of Eden. In Japan a sword is one of the three Imperial treasures, along with a mirror and a handful of jewels. The imperial swords are kept in an adytum, the innermost sanctuary of the temple.

Mr Urashima was beginning to worry about my flight back to Sapporo, but Mr Kinoshita now seemed reluctant to let us go. He went again to his cupboard, and drew from it a bolt of red silk. Again, he knelt, and like a priest performing a ritual of great significance, unwound the silk, laid it aside with a gesture of grave formality, took hold of the *tang*, the spike of roughly finished iron that projected from the scabbard, and with his other hand slowly and tenderly pulled away the wooden sheath from the sword that it protected. Then, with both hands on the *tang*, he slowly lifted up the blade, as the priest at a Christian mass lifts the host and held it away from him upright, at full arm's length. The thicker, shoulder edge of the sword was a matt, rough grey, but the icy blade was almost white, while a ruffle of wind appeared to draw a wave along the whole of its length.

As Mr Kinoshita fixed his eyes on the blade I thought of Charles I on the scaffold, in Marvell's "Horatian Ode", who "with his keener eye / The axe's edge did try". A mysterious change had come over Mr Kinoshita, and it would have been worth missing half a dozen planes to witness it. His heavy and until then unhappy features were transfigured and became beautiful. His eyes both tested the sword and rested on it with a look of reverence and affection, as if he and the sword shared a lover's secret. It was the look of one who knew that whoever might one day handle the sword, his were the hands that had forged it: their bond was unbreakable. We might as well not have been there. At the same time his loneliness seemed to drop off his back like a loosely discarded coat. We saw a creator regarding his creation, and seeing it was good. He slid the sword back into its wooden scabbard, rebound it with its scarf of red silk, and replaced it in the cupboard. We stood up and thanked him as well as we could. On the door-step he smiled again. It was not the smile that he had given the sword, nor the smile of a man glad to be rid of unwelcome visitors; it was a smile of pure and tender sweetness. I hoped he had a friend who loved him.

Hiroshi Doi, painter

Spoken Japanese is notably rich in homophones, words that sound alike but whose meanings differ. While this is a fertile source of puns, it can lead to confusion. When the word is written down, however, the meaning is clear: the *kanji* characters are unambiguous. In conversation, should a listener mistake the meaning of a spoken word, the speaker will trace the *kanji* with his finger on the palm of his hand, and ambiguities are resolved at once. The man who coined the name "Hokkaido" intended it to stand for "the home of the northern people", but as this might have suggested the indigenous Ainu, and as the land was in the process of being settled by Japanese farmers from lands to the south, the government board responsible for administering the island, the *Kaitakushi*, changed its meaning while conserving its sound. The kanji characters for the island of Hokkaido now read, innocuously, "North Sea Way".

On a map Hokkaido looks like a pair of lozenges, one large and one small, north and south, with a boot that resembles the toe of Italy. The high mountains that form the core of each lozenge are kept from drifting further apart by the Tokachi plain, holding them together like a flap of skin. To the east of the plain, the long tail of the Hidaka mountain range stretches down from the island's central massif to Hokkaido's southern tip, Cape Erimo; to the east of the range, the Tokachi river runs in a southerly direction through the plain towards the Pacific ocean. This is the island's richest region of farmland: at ground level, farms of two or three fields deep lie on either side of straight narrow roads that are laid out across the plain in a wide-ranging grid. Although the plain may at first appear spacious, it does not take long to reach the foothills to the south-east. Here the lower hills take on a flatter profile and small enclaves of cultivated land sit on small birch-barricaded plateaux.

Soon after we set off from Obihiro to make for one of these lonely farms, Mr Urashima turned south off the road to Kushiro, a little east of Makubetsu, a small town of farmsteads on the south-eastern edge of the Tokachi plain. We took a farm track of earth and grit between open fields towards a low ridge with plantations of larch that were woven like bands of gold through the dun warp of leafless oaks. The track then climbed diagonally through the woods and came out on a stretch of small, snow-spread fields, smudged with copses of older trees that had been left to themselves when the land was first cleared by the settler-farmers, while recently planted windbreaks of larch and silver birch looked like strokes of ink brushed in against the snow.

Here, on their own isolated plateau, Hiroshi Doi and his wife lived remote from the world, without neighbours. Mr Doi had been born here, and when we visited him the lonely farm had been his home for the following sixty years. His grandfather had been one of the soldier-farmers who had settled in Hokkaido; his father had been a small boy when they had come up from Honshu a century before. While the farmhouse might not have been as old, the greyish-green barns had the look of buildings that have been left out in the snow for many years. As we turned into the yard, we saw through a window the back of Mr Doi's head; through a window to his left, he could look south over fields to a belt of trees; a yew close to the house and couple of ash trees framed his view. He had once worked his fields with a team of horses, but now they lay underneath the fields that they had used to plough. Although he and his wife had bought a tractor to replace them, he could not forget them, nor would he have wished to, for out of the images that lived on in his mind he had painted them in all their beauty and strength, which was why Mr Urashima had taken me to meet him.

Even if Mr Doi had been able to maintain his team of horses, he would not have been able to drive them, for only his head and his hands were free: the postman delivered letters through the window, hand to hand. Mr Doi had never been able to walk easily, and this weakness in his legs had cut off any hopes that he might have had of moving from primary to secondary school, so his formal education had ended almost before it had begun. Thereafter, the limits of the farm were more or less the limits of his physical world. Yet, even as a crippled child, he had learned how to manage his father's horses, and had been fit enough to take over the farm when his father died. He had married and had children of his own, and when in his forties his legs finally failed him, he built pieces of apparatus that enabled him to haul himself about the place.

For a while he continued to farm, relying on the great strength that he had developed in his arms, until all that, too, proved more than he could manage. His wife had kept part of the farm going, but they had had at last to give up most of it, along with the horses. The children had now left home, and on Mr Doi's death, the farm would pass into other hands, or lie abandoned.

Mr Doi, however, had not turned his face to the wall: he had found in his lost horses the freedom to give rein to his own still urgent energies. When he told us that the eyes of a horse are more beautiful than the eyes of a woman, his wife's eyes filled with tears. They were not tears of resentment or jealousy: they were tears of love and pride. If there was pain, it was the pain that she felt for her husband's loss of what he had loved. He had spent years with his animals, brushing down their weighty flanks, their thighs like tree-trunks, their buttocks like apples, their barrelled chests. He had watched how their tails lifted in the wind as they ran, how they dipped their heads towards each other; he had learned to avoid their heavy hoofs. His memory was stocked with these images, and it was out of his memory that he had drawn the creatures that had taken charge of his paintings. Although he had had little training in the arts of *sumi-e*, "drawing with ink", he had taught himself the craft by practising the techniques of *shodo*, "the way of the brush". His horses now charged in their hundreds across endless steppes of paper, rolled up and stored on shelves all over the house, sometimes a squadron, sometimes a brigade. You felt that at any moment you were likely to be trampled under their hooves. They must have galloped through his nights as they thundered through his days.

I visited Mr Doi twice. On the first occasion I feared that he might be overwhelmed by those thousands of charging beasts. On my second visit, a year after the first, I found that he had extended his range: he had painted a human head, the familiar face of Daruma, a Japanese Mr Punch, the eyes glinting, the nose quivering in anticipation of a scandal; he had begun to paint landscapes on gauze that looked like etchings. He had just finished a pre-lapsarian version of *Animal Farm*, where the horse lay down with the lamb and a snake was coiled innocently

between the hoofs of a cow; and he was in the process of painting the animals of the Chinese twelve-year cycle, the cycle that
begins with the year of the rat and ends with the year of the boar.
He had begun to work on a scale hardly larger than a grain of
sand, so that to study the paintings you would have needed a
magnifying glass. His brushes and ink were at his side; rolls of
recent work wrapped in sleeves of newspaper were stacked on
shelves within reach of his left hand. He used hooked sticks to
draw curtains or pick up any paper that he had let fall. He could
pull a table at his right to fit over his knees. What he was not
able to reach, his wife would fetch. His futon lay at his feet, and
he worked at three o'clock in the afternoon, or at three o'clock in
the morning. If he had visitors, he had time enough to make up
for time he had lost.

In *Zen and the Fine Arts* Shin'ichi Hisamatsu sets out the seven
principles of Zen aesthetics. The first of these is asymmetry:
this principle states that since symmetry is perfection, it has
no place in such an imperfect world as ours, which is why the
layout of a Zen temple is asymmetrical. The second principle is
the simplicity of the unadorned line. The third is austerity, an
irregularity that enables us to recognise the skeleton beneath the
flesh. The fourth is naturalness, a line that is unstrained, with at
least the appearance of artless grace. The fifth principle is subtle
profundity and deep reserve, the awareness of what has been
left out. The sixth is freedom from attachment, not only attachment to worldly things, but also to the Divine Being itself. And
the seventh – should we reach this stage – is the emptiness of
ultimate tranquillity.

Mr Doi had observed, by instinct or experience, the principle
of subtle profundity, the art of knowing what to leave out; and he
had become the master of the simple line, the swift stroke of the

brush that implies all that has not been represented, the parts of the picture that are not drawn. I doubted, however, that he had arrived, or ever would arrive, at the final stages of spiritual progress, freedom from worldly attachments, and thence ultimate tranquillity. Makers of every kind seem to be haunted by a compulsion that prevents them from ever giving up their devotion to the practice of their art.

Only twice, and only on my second visit, did I catch Mr Doi's eye, and I did not feel altogether comfortable: there was a fierceness in his regard that was not easy to face. As his reputation had by this time begun to spread, he had allowed his hair, now turning white, to grow, along with his beard, in the ancient style. He looked like a figure from Japanese cultural history, a sage, venerable and wise; but he did not look as if he would be an easy man to live with, not a man who would, by any natural inclination, have chosen to sit still. His arms and neck were still thick and heavily muscled, as smooth as a wrestler's. His eyes had a bird's quickness and acuity; but they were the eyes of a falcon, not a dove.

Yeats' poem "Lapis Lazuli" describes a semi-precious stone on which three old men are depicted climbing towards a teahouse; they are wise and sad with the weight of a sorrowful world, but they are not cast down, for all the sorrow that they have looked upon:

> On all the tragic scene they stare...
> Their eyes, mid many wrinkles, their eyes,
> Their ancient, glittering eyes, are gay.

Mr Doi's eyes struck me as looking like that: not the eyes of a man who is afraid, nor of a man who is likely to turn his cheek for a second blow.

He reminded me, too, of the eponymous hero of Sophocles' play *Philoctetes*. Philoctetes is a disabled princeling with a priceless gift, a master archer crippled by a wound in his heel that gives off so offensive a smell that his companions, on their way to the plains of Troy, abandon him on a deserted island. But Philoctetes is also the possessor of an invincible bow, bequeathed to him by Herakles, who received it from Apollo, the god of music and healing, the god who leads the dance of the nine muses. He is the archetype, says the American critic Edmund Wilson in *The Wound and the Bow*, of a particular kind of artist, if not indeed of all great artists. Wilson takes the story of the wounded archer with the magic bow as the epitome of the artist: a man who is both cursed and rewarded. We may note, in passing, that Hephaestus, god of blacksmiths and other craftsmen, was also a cripple, as was his Roman successor, Vulcan.

I said that Mr Doi's eyes reminded me of a bird of prey, and a line from T. S. Eliot's "Little Gidding" comes to mind: "the spirit unappeased and peregrine". Mr Doi had a spirit not easily appeased, and I wondered if even the active life of a farmer would, in the end, have been enough to satisfy and salve it. In the middle of his life, he had had to learn the techniques of a new craft and a new kind of manual dexterity. Would he, I wondered, have traded his paintings he made for the ability to walk in the evening around fields that he had ploughed with his team of horses? When he wished to move, he had, with his arms, to manoeuvre himself onto the floor, to lie down on his back, and with his elbows lever himself along. He had to do it while we were with him. This might have been too embarrassing to watch were it not that, unlike Philoctetes, Mr Doi showed no self-pity. It was a fact of his life, and if he could do it without flinching, so should those who saw him. It was with some apprehension that I decided to ask him – or ask Mr Urashima to ask him – how much he felt that he owed to his wife. But Mr Doi did not appear in the least put out by the question: ninety per cent, he answered.

Wordsworth, contemplating a bust of Newton, wrote that Newton had voyaged through "strange seas of thought alone". It struck me, as I left his farm, that Mr Doi, almost as immobile as Newton with his marble face, and able to move only with the greatest difficulty, had travelled through his art further than most of those who in our age of international travel unthinkingly circumnavigate the globe.

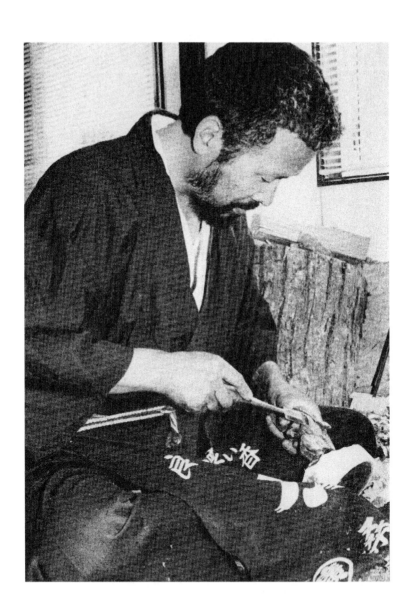

Ryudo Nagao, wood-carver

S apporo is a young city, and traces of the Ainu, its autoch-
thonous inhabitants, are everywhere; the name "Sapporo"
is itself an Ainu word, meaning "bed of a dry river". On
the campus of Hokkaido University stake-posts in a grassy
clearing of giant Japanese alders I used to visit mark the site of
a long-abandoned Ainu village. They reminded me of a grove
in a wood of English oaks. Ainu fabrics were once woven from
bark; their cloth tunics are still banded with appliqué designs,
indigo on beige linen, or the same colours reversed; the designs
are abstract, symmetrical, and to the untutored eye look vaguely
Aztec; hangings are woven in bands of green, red and indigo,
colours that Ainu derive from local plants. They still wear traditional garments on the occasions when, with impassive patience,
they dance for a tourist audience.

In central Sapporo, visitors crowd the shops of Tanuki-koji,
a ten-block arcade where they can buy Ainu artefacts carved in
local wood. The tanuki is a racoon-like animal whose images
stand upright at the doors of places to dine, with weighty testi-
cles and a stubby penis that is only rarely covered with an apron.
It belongs to a culture older than the one Japan imposed on the

island that it had colonised not so long before. The figures in wood that visitors to Tanuki-koji buy as souvenirs tend to be standardised and identical: a profile of a young woman and a young man in relief on a panel, a free-standing bear with a salmon in its mouth. They can be bought, too, in places where the Ainu still live in reservations, such as the one at Akan, perhaps the most popular of the Ainu villages of the tourist trail, near a large lake in the east of the island, surrounded by wooded volcanic hills, and the centre of the Akan National Park.

If you approach Akan from the north, you cross the Bihoro Pass and see below you what might strike a visitor from Britain as a Japanese version of Lake Windermere or Loch Ness. Coming from the west you drive through miles of still primeval and mostly deciduous forest, passing through Ashoro, a large village at the north-east corner of the Tokachi Plain, where the pastures begin to buckle and break up into shallow valleys, stitched and braided with trees that were left standing when the land was first cleared. On a bitterly cold day in early April Mr Urashima drove us here – myself, a young American teaching for a short while at his language school, and a photographer friend of the man whom we were going to see – a woodcarver named Ryudo Nagao.

Mr Nagao had been born in Ashoro, and when we visited him he had lived there for all of his thirty-eight years; though his hair and beard were going grey, his face was as smooth as a boy's, his complexion as fresh. He was one of the three best woodcarvers in Hokkaido, he told us, and during his short professional career had been remarkably successful: he had sold every piece that he made. When he had sold one, he said, he never wanted to see it again. He recognised only two rival carvers, but he did not tell us who they were. He did tell us that we were lucky to catch him in good spirits, as he had been in a bad mood for the last couple of months. That he was to remain in a genial humour throughout our visit was not luck, though, for Mr Urashima is a genial man and promotes geniality in others.

Mr Nagao's house, which he had designed himself, was an ingenious arrangement of small spaces without doors that opened off each other at different levels, so that while the square yardage cannot have been great and the house was full of stuff, it did not appear over-crowded. The main living area – where tall, angled windows faced south and east, flanking a Scandinavian stove – was narrow but lofty, and felt almost spacious: a couple of steps led up to the kitchen, while steps the other way led down to the hall and a small workroom, which was empty apart from a tatami mat and a row of tools lined up on the floor alongside. We had been told that Mr Nagao was a motor racing enthusiast, and several ancient racing cars were placed about the lawn outside like pieces of modern sculpture, but we had not been prepared for the three elderly motorbikes in the living room, set on plinths at different levels, each with assorted embellishments: one wore a pair of goggles on its headlamps, gold watches draped the handlebars of another, while the third was being used as a clothes horse; I thought of Richard Wilbur's poem "Museum Piece":

> *Edgar Degas purchased once*
> *A fine el Greco which he kept*
> *Against the wall beside the bed*
> *To hang his pants on while he slept.*

A telephone hung on the wall amongst ancient guitars, a violin, and several storm lanterns; an old sewing machine was attended by a gramophone and a pre-war grocer's scales, its pan a fruit bowl. Someone would have had to do a lot of dusting, and we had been told that Mr Nagao's wife had recently left him. I

wondered if this had been partly why. I had an odd sense of foreboding. Since he had very few of his pieces for us to see, we had
to be content with photographs, which he was ready to show us:
convoluted dragons, articulated insects, a man drawing water
from a well, a man pulling a rickshaw, bears fishing, bowls of
fruit, and a wonderful Blakean tiger, its stripes the ribs of the
wood, the wood grain forming the muscles of its neck. Since *ryu*
is the word for dragon, Ryudo Nagao had chosen the dragon as
his tutelary spirit: photographs of his pieces showed it in all its
labyrinthine ins and outs. His carvings seemed to capture the
energies of the animals themselves: a bear, its muscles tautening
as it reached out to seize a rabbit, the rabbit's haunches tight-
ening as it strove to escape, or a harpooner's arm flexing as he
drew back his barbed shaft before launching it at a salmon. If the
works in the gift-shops were dead wood, these ones appeared, at
least in photographs, to be alive.

Mr Nagao had come to his craft late, one of several craftsmen
we met who had fallen into their chosen occupation by a happy
accident. After his first adult employment as a garage attendant,
he went through a score of jobs until, in his late twenties, he saw
a programme on television of sculptors working with wood. He
had always enjoyed drawing and painting, but as he watched
it came to him as a revelation that this was what he had been
waiting for. If you suddenly see that you must be a worker in
wood, you still have to learn your trade, and Mr Nagao joined a
local guild or corporation of carvers, but after only six months he
left: he was unable to accept being reduced to an automaton at
a factory bench. He had quite soon found buyers for his pieces,
he said, collectors who were looking for craftsmanship with an
individual approach. So, I asked, where did his ideas come from?
From the wood itself, he said. When he held a piece of virgin

timber in his hand he had no prior conception of what he would find: there was no picture in his mind's eye. He allowed his hands to explore the power of the wood, the forms locked up within the wood's carapace, then to reveal them with his adze: if his hands found out a tree, the lines of the carved tree followed the upward thrust of the tree from which the wood had come, the veins of leaves figured in the tree-rings; if he found the shapes of men or of animals, the muscles and sinews drew their bulk from the thews and sinews of the tree.

He used three types of wood for three different types of work. One, the Japanese yew, *onko*, tough and smooth, is suitable for small and intricate pieces; you can work inside it, Mr Nagao explained, to make birdcages and lobster pots without breaking its bones, leaving the fowl or the fish inside their coops or cages without a flaw or a defect, all fashioned from a single piece of wood. The wood of the pagoda tree, *enju*, he said, is also good for small objects, especially those that simulate the textures and colours of the wood itself. For the Ainu it has a particular virtue, as the laurel tree had once for the Celts: if planted close to a dwelling, its benign presence protects the home and its inhabitants from harmful spirits. When freshly cut, *enju* does not smell very wholesome, but its firm and pinkish flesh, growing white towards the edges, makes it ideal for objects that need to be subtle and intricate: from its tendons Mr Nagao had set free small insects and little men, the mythical figures of Ainu folk culture. Finally, the wood of the tree that botanists call *Kalopanax* and the Japanese call *sen* is suited to large panels in relief: although its texture is soft, Mr Nagao chose it for such solid objects as rocks, animals, and men; the background panels remain rough-hewn, while the forms detach or disengage themselves from the wood's restraining ligatures, like captives in a sculpture by Michelangelo, struggling to escape from their marble bandages.

As the day of our visit happened to be my birthday, Mr Nagao offered me a gift, and I selected a larger than life-sized cricket made of enju wood, The cricket rests on the leaf of a mountain grape, *yamabudo*; a bunch of grapes is tucked underneath the foliage. On the day I was given it, the grapes were white, while the leaf and the cricket were both the colour of watered Burgundy; since then, however, the colours have faded to a uniform brown. One of the cricket's antennae was cocked over its shoulder in a quirky, risky gesture; the other pointed ahead, and while I was dusting it one day it broke off. I reflected that an injury such as this might well have been its fate had it been a living cricket, so this did not matter too much. Nor, I fancy, would Mr Nagao have minded.

Mr Nagao had told us that he was a difficult man to live with, and I thought of a remark in Tom Stoppard's play *Travesties*: "For every thousand people, there's nine hundred doing the work, ninety doing well, nine doing good, and one lucky bastard who's the artist". I wondered if Ryudo Nagao thought of himself as lucky in this respect. It was clear that he met the definition of an artist in Stoppard's play: "someone who is gifted in some way that enables him to do something more or less well which can only be done badly or not at all by someone who is not thus gifted". And it is true that artists may enjoy freedom from certain duties obligatory in other citizens. But they are not free of the obligation to stick to their last, to ensure that their work is as well done as they can make it. And the lucky accident that turns people into artists may entail a temperament that can be hard to live with – both for artists themselves and for those who live with them. Yet the work may justify the life: as W. H. Auden wrote of the controversial French playwright Paul Claudel. Time, wrote Auden, "... will pardon Paul Claudel, / Pardons him for writing well." It does not follow, though, that if you wish to be an artist you have to be a bastard, or that if you are a bastard then you are likely to be so much the better artist.

As we drove away from Ashoro, we passed timber-yards with tree-trunks stacked vertically under tarpaulin sheets, some freshly felled, the sawn-off ends pink and creamy, while the timber in other stacks was dark with the weather of several winters. It would all one day be used for the frames of new houses, even small apartment blocks, for however modern the exterior cladding and the interior arrangements, such buildings still rest upon a basic wooden scaffolding. The Japanese have retained their ancient passion for wood and its products. You see it in the stacks of wooden beams as you walk past a site where a new house is going up, or in the department stores where wooden bowls and boxes, polished or lacquered, line shelves alongside the ceramic ware. We could perhaps say that the Japanese handle wood as Chardin handled paint, as an end in its itself rather than a means to some other end.

Back in my hotel room, I took my cricket out of its wrappings, and let the leaf on which it stood rest on my hand: a gift from its maker's hand to mine. It seemed that Mr Nagao had succeeded in embracing his vocation as an artist. Yet my sense of foreboding while we were at his house had not been without reason: a year or two later, Mr Urashima told me that Mr Nagao's commercial contacts had been so demanding, so avaricious, that he had disappeared, no one knew where.

Chiyoji Asahara, glass-blower

I met Mr Urashima in Sapporo and we caught a train to Otaru, forty minutes away to the north-west. Halfway there, the railway line meets the sea, and follows the coast. On the right we had a view of promontories and, rising out of the sea, finger-shaped stalagmites of rock; on the left small fishing villages huddled below the cliffs. On that day, their crevices were stuffed with snow, and the sea was grey with foam. Otaru is not a large city, and though Mr Urashima knew where to go, he did not know how to get there; nor did our taxi driver, who dropped us at a junction in despair.

"It will take you five minutes", said a passer-by. Ten minutes later, another passer-by directed us to take a road that rose towards Mount Tengu, high to our left. After ten more minutes we reached the crest of the road at the point where swaying gondolas take skiers to the top of the mountain. Here, finally, rooted into the hill-side like a pillbox or small fortress, battleship grey, was the place we had come to visit. At the side of the road across from the ski-lift, Mr Chiyoji Asahara's glass studio is a hexagonal building reached by a footbridge from the car park. Should a visitor wonder why the studio was built in so defensive a style, as if to guard the approaches to the pass, the reason becomes clear as soon as you enter. The building is designed from the inside out. The entrance hall forms half of the hexagon and is set above a store room; glass cabinets built against the inner walls as in a gallery display the master's work, while tables are stacked with less precious glass that you can buy at the counter; the northern half of the hexagon rises through both storeys, and from an open balustrade in the gallery you can look down at the glass-workers in the space below. Clerestory windows provide the main light, while windows at either side offer views of the hills across a valley to the west and towards the ski slopes on the right. Tall narrow windows overlook the port of Otaru, now far away beneath, the hillsides on either side hemming it in, the sea beyond.

Chiyoji Asahara is a native of Osaka, whose inhabitants are widely admired in Japan for their friendliness. He has an excellent command of English and was eager to tell us without being asked about the glories of glass. His family had been glass-blowers for four generations; his father's workshop had employed 150 men; but as the workshop was now in the hands of his brother, he had been free to look around for a site where he might set up on his own. Otaru is a long way from Osaka, but it is far less humid, and glass-blowing is hot work. Although Otaru already supported a maker of glass, also called Asahara, Chiyoji welcomed competition, and Otaru, once run down and fearful of its future, has become a major tourist attraction, for which the glassworks may take much of the credit.

Glass, Mr Asahara told us, can be made anywhere: the same type of furnace, the same materials. Unlike a potter, whose life is made much easier if his clay is close to hand, a glass-blower has little trouble transporting the necessary ingredients: silica, lime, soda, and a number of metal oxides if the glass is to be coloured.

A benign climate and the tempo of provincial life are helpful. They are more suited to the rhythms of artistic creation than the hurry of life in a big city. He had chosen Otaru rather some other city in Hokkaido because it could never grow: a tight crescent of hills holds it as if with a pair of pliers. It will remain modest and manageable, said Mr Asahara, its flora and fauna beyond the reach of the developers who are despoiling other scenic parts of the island. Here, he could draw inspiration from green woods in the summer, white hillsides in the winter, the scarlet of autumn leaves, and the rainbows over the water in the bay.

The techniques of glass-blowing have hardly changed since Syrian craftsmen invented the blowing-iron some time before the birth of Christ, and blowing glass requires little further in the way of equipment. Years before I came to Japan, I visited the Mdina Glassworks in Valletta, in Malta, where glass-making is centuries old. What I saw in Otaru, where the practice of glass-making is only just beginning to make a name for itself, seemed much the same, although the Mdina glassworks were housed in a space as large as an aircraft hangar, while the austere working area of the Otaru glassworks suggested a monastic chapter house, a calm and consecrated space.

Three barrel-like furnaces stood on brick plinths; a small cooling shed stood between the north-facing windows; three benches, set like tables beside a dentist's chair, were each laid with no more than a pair of shears and a pair of callipers; close by, iron bars rested on trestles at waist height: everything was at hand, orderly, ready for use. Although Mr Asahara had seven apprentices, only three could work at any one time. On the day of our visit they were making stemmed glasses. After the blower had withdrawn his blowing-iron from the furnace, a molten bulb wobbling at its end, he carried the rod to one of the benches, giving it an occasional puff on the way, twirling it constantly to prevent the force of gravity from dragging the emerging bud earthwards. He then laid the rod on one of the horizontal bars, rolling it on the bar with one hand, while with the other he took a pair of shears to shape the glass; sometimes he exchanged the shears for the callipers to check the size, but mostly he trusted his eye. When he was satisfied, he held the glass with the shears and with a sharp tap detached it from the blowing-iron. One of the other apprentices was standing by with another blob of molten glass on its own iron; this he pressed to the base of the now fully opened bloom and moulded it with his shears into an attenuated stem; he then rubbed the base of the stem with a folded newspaper to flatten and smooth it; finally, he placed the completed glass in the small shed between the windows to cool.

The young men might have been servers at an altar, as they wove back and forth from furnace to bench, and from second furnace to second bench. They appeared to take no notice of one another, yet at exactly the moment a contribution was required each would be where he needed to be. Although they were making routine pieces, each would be unique, each glass or bowl or jug would have its own character. If Chiyoji Asahara was satisfied with it, it would go on show in the shop, where he hoped that someone on the way out would buy it, for, though he had no hesitation in calling himself an artist, he was also a man of business, with a young family to bring up and a mortgage to pay off. And since he was a business man, he was forced to spend more time on business than on blowing. He was conscious, too, of his obligations to his successors, for though at the time we met him he was only in his early forties, his father had died at the age of 48, and his own mortality, he told us, was never far from his mind.

Unlike most of the other craftsmen I was to meet, Chiyoji Asahara had been born to his craft, with a blowing iron in his mouth, so to speak. He had entered his father's workshop in his early twenties, and had first exhibited his work in 1975 at the Kanagawa Museum of Modern Art. A year later he had gone to London to attend a seminar and had there met two men who were to give him confidence in his own approach to his work, while also influencing how he would come to understand and speak about it. Harry Littleton and Dominic Labino were revolutionaries in the world of glass-blowing, for they insisted that whoever designs a piece of glass must also be the one who blows it: for this reason they called themselves glass artists. It had not occurred to me that pieces of glass might be designed by someone who thought of himself as an artist but be blown by an artisan, and Mr Asahara abhorred the practice: the glass should be the work of one pair of hands, he said, from start to finish.

He had strong views, too, about artists' responsibility to express and share their gifts. Should you deny or misuse your gift, he said, you would be damned ("damned" was the English word that he used). Yet, I reflected, should your gift be for glass-blowing, and should you live in an eastern country, you will have been unlikely until recently to have had much chance to express it. Although the Chinese had at times made objects in glass, these had been coarse and clumsy. In the East, said Mr Asahara, people have always had a rather poor opinion of glass and its potentialities: they have been ignorant of its history and indifferent to its merits. That was all changing. Museums were holding exhibitions of modern glass and some coffee shops were embellished as if in homage to Lalique and Tiffany. Since Mr Asahara was keen to speed up this process, it was perhaps fitting that he should have come to Hokkaido, to the land of pioneers, to do it, although in his own eyes he was less a pioneer than a missionary.

He was even, he told us, on a crusade – again, "crusade" was the word he used – to challenge the pre-eminence of ceramics in Japanese tradition and cultural life. This, he argued, applied to the tea ceremony specifically: as windows once made of paper are now made of glass, and chopsticks that are traditionally made of wood are occasionally made of glass, too, why should not the utensils for the tea ceremony also be made of glass?

Mr Asahara had something to say, too, about the artist as athlete, the need for perfect coordination of hand and eye, and in the case of glass-blowing, the control of breathing. The practice of a craft entails, like any athletic performance, establishing a rhythm, and a craftsman depends upon knowing how to breathe, though different tasks require different techniques and rhythms. Where a singer must fill the back of the rib-cage as, for example, the mezzo-soprano Christa Ludwig does to carry her through the long, unbroken phrases of Schubert's "Ganymed", the glass-blower, like an oboist, will fill his cheeks with air and release it, not for a sustained Aeolian exhalation but in quick cherubic puffs. He judges the scale and volume of his glass, which he shapes with his breath, from within. A glass-blower enters his work with his breath, as God enters creation in the Book of Genesis, bringing to life what was inchoate. Glass, Mr Asahara argued, is not mere matter: it has its own sources of energy, like the potter's clay. You must respond to it with tact: stroke it with courtesy, speak to it gently. If you do not, it may well come to pieces in your hands.

Since Mr Asahara had, like Mr Nagao the woodcarver, been able to sell most of his work, he had little in the display cases around the walls for us to see. Although there were photographs,

photographs cannot give you a sense of size or scale. One reason why many Japanese are still suspicious of glass is that if you drop it, it will break; I have a friend who even today will not have anything made of glass in his house. Yet Mr Asahara's pieces looked weighty and well-shaped, as if safe enough to handle. Within the body of the glass currents of colour undulated like channels of oceanic water moving through the sea lanes; a branch extended a leafy arm around the body of a glass as if it were embracing it; autumnal leaves lay scattered where they had fallen.

Mr Asahara hoped that whoever handled his work would appreciate its unique features. He wished us to understand that when glass is mass-produced, rolled out in sheets, its vital elements are lost. Hand-blown glass is by its nature mobile and vigorous, even tough. "Glass", said Mr Asahara, "is arrested fire". He had no doubt that it was his gift to release the living elements of glass. Neither wood nor clay inspired him, nor wool nor ink, nor the etcher's plate nor the engraver's block. Only glass would do. He spoke of *kanseihin*, completeness, a term that was new to me but vitally important to him, which he used to refer to a work that was finished and complete in itself, the consequence of a unity established between the maker and the thing that he or she has made, the oneness of creators and their creations. This was an idea that could refer as well to Mr Kinoshita, the swordsmith, and his sword, or works that endure long after their makers are dead, even as far back as those who lived before history, in the age of Jomon culture, those makers whose names will never have been recorded and might never have been known.

Yuriko Oido, etcher

From my living room in Sapporo I look west across roofs towards wooded hills that are little more than a minute away, if you are a crow. In early May, the woods begin to fill out in tightly bunched cobbles of green leaf; in December, after the first snows have fallen, the trees stand up in silhouette along the crests like bristles on a boar's back, or as darker bands against the undulating folds of the higher hills beyond, or are hatched against the rising ground of the ribs of the hills like the marks left on a print by the etcher's needle. On just such a day of wintery black on white, I met Mr Urashima at his hotel in Sapporo, this time to visit a craftswoman very much closer to home, at least to my home. Yet I had no idea where we were going until the taxi dropped us at a gate in a high hedge of yew at the roadside. Then I saw that we were not far from the point where, on Sundays in the spring or autumn, after I had walked down through the woods from the summit of Mount Moiwa, the path came out on a road in the village of Fushimi, where the land rises in afforested hillsides that even the settler-farmers would not have attempted to reclaim. In the dying light of a summer afternoon, I would walk down through the wood, its lower slopes a sombre forest darkened by heavy-limbed trees, their obtruding roots calling to mind a drawing by the English book illustrator Arthur Rackham.

A number of houses designed by architects have recently eased their way into the shadowy flank of the hills here, but older houses line the road, one-storey settlers' homes that now hide behind thick hedges of mature yew. Yuriko Oido had been born in an older house further down the road, but when she was ten her parents had moved to her current home, where since their deaths she had lived alone for thirty-five years. We had to clamber up a bank of snow to reach her front door and could see that she did not spend much time clearing the path. Nor did she spend much money on keeping her house warm. She had begun to draw, she told us, when she was four, and the years from then until she was nine and living still in the old settler-built *tonden* house with her family had been her most prolific. She later attended the local College of Education, only a little further down the road, and not far from the ropeway station for the cars that carry you to the top of Mount Moiwa.

I knew the College well, since for six years I had worked there one day a week, and at a coffee shop nearby had bought the first of my Sakata pots, the master of the shop an acquaintance of Mr Urashima and Mr Sakata. The College buildings were New England clapboard, like many Hokkaido schools built at the end of the nineteenth century; the classrooms smelled of wood dust, and the walls, a little shabby, were the colour of old honey; the light was filtered by the trees that grew close to the windows in the courtyard around which the wooden buildings had been ranged. Here, Ms Oido had spent her student years learning how to paint with oils, but while still a student she had also come across the craft of etching, and as this was a medium that appeared to suit her love of drawing, she decided to learn how to etch. As soon as she graduated, she visited anyone who practised the craft, and picked up whatever they could teach her; but she never learned in a systematic way, did not sit at the feet of a master, and was therefore not beholden to the disciplines of a formal school: she learned her craft, as van Dyke and Rembrandt had done in their day, by practice, and by learning from her mistakes.

What attracted her from the start was the suitability of etching as a method of drawing, a style that requires clarity of contour and elasticity of line. Engraving, similarly, is a linear art and can achieve marvellous effects of light and shade, but she had found that etching was a method that seemed even more suited to what she wished to draw, the ordinary people of rural Hokkaido, the chubby-cheeked descendants of the *tonden-hei* and other settlers. While the pictures suggest the world of her childhood and of her parents, farmers and fishermen, the markets and meetings that celebrated the rituals of lives lived by the season, she insisted that she drew only what she saw, not what she remembered or had imagined. At the same time, etching is a suitable technique if you wish to make your living as a book illustrator, which was how Ms Oido made hers. Just before we visited her, one of her books, *Big Arubesu and I*, had won a prize; another was almost ready for the publisher.

Ms Oido's subjects are people, women all of them, and middle-aged. While the background may be vistas of village streets, trees, fields, farm-buildings, stacks of wood, and though the foreground may display piles of vegetables on tables in a small-town market, the faces are what matter: bucolic and plain, round-cheeked and snub-nosed, they are reminiscent of old Dutch faces in paintings by members of the Brueghel family or Hieronymus Bosch; they reminded me, too, of Stanley Spencer's paintings of Cookham Dene in the Royal County of Berkshire.

Ms Oido, however, insisted that no one had influenced her except the people whose faces she drew so lovingly. Her vision was hers and hers alone; her teacher had been the medium itself and the need to be true to what she could see in front of her; nothing else mattered.

While I did not feel that I could ask Ms Oido directly if she could tell us why the people in her paintings meant so much to her, I felt that I could put a question or two about the craft, the answers to which might, indirectly, tell us why she drew these particular people with such tender care. Was she consciously aware that people attracted her more than trees, for instance? Did she have any message that she might have been trying to communicate through her drawings that could have been expressed in words as well as in a drawing? Or was she drawing merely to please herself?

Yes, she drew to please herself, she said. She made it clear that she did not think any of the other questions were worth even bothering about. I remarked that many painters painted, as many writers wrote, to preserve something that had mattered to them, some aspect of their lives that they did not wish to see disappear for ever, but to leave as a record for future generations: to capture, as in a painting of cherry blossom, the ephemeral beauty of their own times, not because it was *their* life and times, but because they did not want something that had seemed beautiful to them to be obliterated forever. Perhaps she wished to say something to the unborn generations of Hokkaido children about the lives of their ancestors?

No, she said, it was nothing like that, either. She was firm about this. She drew pictures of these particular people in these particular settings quite simply for the pleasure that it gave her to do so: a pleasure that left her feeling perfectly satisfied and

content, and she saw no need for any other kind of justifica-
tion. Although others might take pleasure in her drawings, she
simply wished to enter into the being of the people she drew;
she wished to live inside these women as if by drawing them
she could become them. Since Ms Oido does not live in the rural
world that she depicts, I supposed that she meant to inhabit it
imaginatively, but, no, I was wrong about that, too; her desires
were purely physical: the women in her drawings have round
faces that, when coloured, are rubicund, as featureless as apples:
Ms Oido hoped that one day her face would grow not only to
resemble their faces, but become one of them.

Making is a process of becoming as well as a process of understanding, and I found myself wondering what might be going on
when the two become fused, as it does with the greatest artists
and writers – Shakespeare, Mozart, Chardin. It can also happen
in the work of botanical and ornithological painters, where by a
selfless contemplation of a flower or a bird, the artist disappears
and becomes the flower or the bird, and invisibly assumes its
nature. This has an erotic aspect: it seeks, though, not to possess
but rather to become one with the beloved, to be absorbed in its
being. In Book VIII of Milton's *Paradise Lost*, Raphael explains
to Adam that only the angels are able to achieve such a mutual
fusing of selves. So it may be that we turn to the making of sim-
ulacra of things that we love in order to achieve some fragile kind
of symbiosis with them, when such a union with another person
eludes us, as in the fruitless search for the ideal friend.

While Ms Oido and I were talking, I recalled also the work
of the Scottish psychiatrist Ian Suttie, who thought that our
sexual urges are a sublimated form of a longing to caress, that
an emphasis upon sex has made us reluctant to express feelings
of tenderness, that our need to care for a beloved object is more

fundamental than our need for sexual release. I decided to ask Ms Oido if she felt that her gestures as she handled her tools had something of the nature of a caress, as if fondling them as well as handling them. Did she feel that she was laying her hands upon the things that she drew, not to steal them but to bless them?

The questions startled her, but then she smiled: she had never thought of it quite like that, but yes, that was what she felt as she worked. This emboldened me to ask another question. Like myself, Ms Oido is unmarried; and neither of us has a child. Many people, especially in Japan, believe that without offspring we are only partially complete, and they may be right. Yet it is possible for us to see in our work as artists or writers an echo of the fulfilment, the completion, even the consummation, that a parent may feel on the birth of a child. (One of my Japanese friends once said to me "A year ago there was nothing, but this year I am holding my baby daughter in my arms".) I asked Ms Oido if she thought about her work in such terms, as her children. Did she love her old ladies as one might love a child, putting your arms around it tenderly? Did she give them her undivided attention? Did she love them without conditions? Why, yes, of course, she said.

By this stage in my meetings with the craftspeople of Hokkaido I had come to see that before everything else they were in love with their own particular medium. It is the irreducible nature of the medium that the maker wishes to celebrate, whether paint, or musical sounds, or glass, or words. Chardin expresses his love of paint, Mozart his love of music, Michelangelo his love of marble, and so on. When I put this to Ms Oido her answer was another unequivocal yes. She was not trying to record or to tell us anything: she simply loved to draw, and drawing on copper was what she had come to love best. If all that we are anxious to express is ourselves, then no one will be interested; we can only express ourselves if we forget ourselves in whatever medium we have chosen to work in; only then, if we have anything worth saying, will anyone else be willing to listen.

Did Ms Oido have plans for new projects? No, she simply wished to go on doing what she had been doing until then. She worked slowly and there was plenty still to do. Only at the end of our conversation did we talk about the business of etching itself, about the biting with acid into metal. It is not an ancient skill, like the making of pots or the blowing of glass. The first known example of an etching is the work of a German in the sixteenth century who was by trade an armourer. Soon afterwards, Albrecht Dürer tried his hand at it, but as he used iron rather than copper, the results did not encourage him to persevere. His contemporary Albrecht Altdorfer was the first to use the method to depict landscapes, while a younger contemporary Lucas van Leyden was probably the first to use copper rather than iron. Since copper had already been used for engraving, the early workers found that it was possible to combine the two techniques of etching and engraving, the difference being that whereas an engraver digs out the lines directly on wood or metal with a graver, the etcher, having first applied a film of wax or some other acid-resistant coating to the copper surface, scores the wax lightly with a fine needle without marking the copper plate: the weight of the needle itself is often enough to incise the lines in the wax.

An etcher's needles are fixed in wooden handles that are shaped to the hand of each individual etcher, and unlike an engraver's tools, which are pointed and sharp, their points are rounded or blunt. Ms Oido has just half a dozen needles, wrapped in a cloth holdall, the only tools she uses. The plates, though, have to be prepared, and this can be done in the kitchen sink, where they are washed with running water, after which they will be coated with wax, the acid resist, to protect the parts of the metal that are not to be etched. All that she needs for this is a small flame. Once a plate is ready, she sits on the floor to draw, the plate propped against a low wooden bench, and as the baths of acid and the printing press are housed elsewhere, this is the only obvious evidence that her sitting room is her workroom. Ms Oido prepares just five or six plates a year, so she only rarely needs to visit the printing shop, where the plates will first be submerged in acid, which burns into the metal that the lines incised in the wax will have opened up. This process can be repeated as often as the etcher wishes, and further lines can be added at any stage. The more often a plate is dipped in the bath of acid, the more deeply the lines will be etched, so that the most delicate lines will be left until the very end. It is at this final stage that lines can be engraved directly on to the copper plate with a graver, a technique that is known as dry point.

When Ms Oido is satisfied that the drawing is complete she will take prints, and she must surely hope that there are those, whatever she may say to the contrary, who will find something in her work that appeals to them, enough to encourage the publishers who will produce her books and the readers who will buy them. For me, at least, this is not really the women she loves but the completely realised world that the women inhabit. Mr Urashima bought three of Ms Oido's bookplate-sized prints for me to take home. As I sit at my desk I can look at the prints, and look up across the intervening roofs to Mount Moiwa where the woods fall out of sight and where, in her small house behind its tall yew hedge, Ms Oido still draws the faces of those she wishes to become.

Aya Kiuchi, weaver

The landscapes of Hokkaido are almost absurdly photo-genic, the bookshops stocked with albums designed to show off their several beauties: of mountains, rivers and lakes, the cultivated valleys enclosed by deciduous woods of oak, ash and maple, and those species "native to Japan" that I used to see in the Royal Botanic Garden in Edinburgh before I was myself transplanted eastwards. Mountain-birch with weighty trunks and chalk-white bark cover the lower slopes of the hills; fir and pines succeed them higher up; in late April, white anemones and yellow stars of David float upon the snow-soaked leafage of the woodland floors. And if Hokkaido knows nothing of bluebells, the paler tones of corydalis can, if you half-close your eyes for a moment, deceive you. Giant kingcups and skunk cabbage spring up in woodland bogs on their release in April from months locked in the ice; alpines bloom on the treeless lower slopes of the central massif; lavender is grown as a crop; ground phlox is planted to edge farm gardens or on dykes above the boundary ditches; in October, acres of goldenrod take over any land left waste; on the dunes beside the Okhotsk Sea, fields of *Hemerocallis* catch fire. And in autumn, the dark-green woods that line the steep-sided caldera of Lake Mashu, a mysterious body of water that lies in the east of the island on the eastern edge of the Akan National Park, are threaded with bands of crimson, yellow and bronze.

Winters, however, are long, and although the Hokkaido-born boast that the island has four seasons, the spring and autumn are usually over before you have begun to enjoy their long-anticipated arrival. In November, gardeners erect tepees of straw over the topiary to protect the branches from the snow. In February, ice floes crowd the Sea of Okhotsk right up to the shore, and television cameras chart their coming, as they do that of the red-headed cranes, or the arrival of the cherry blossom, which happens five or more weeks after its appearance in western Japan. When the snow ploughs cut through banks of roadside snow in March, you can read in the strata the history of a winter not yet over. Although Hokkaido lies on the same line of latitude as the Riviera, no flowers bloom before April, and the riven slopes of Asahidake, Hokkaido's highest summit, are packed with snow, even in June.

Those who wish to climb Asahidake must pass through Asahikawa, Hokkaido's second city, and as Mr Urashima and I approached from the south-west, we saw our goal set on a low plateau. It looked like a middle-European pre-baroque monastery on an eminence, as if sited there for centuries, except that the materials were clearly contemporary, and we knew that it was not a monastery. The first storey was faced with red brick, while pillars of brick supported the arches of a deep portico; the second storey was plastered and painted white; the grey-blue roof was steeply pitched and pierced with narrow, gabled windows. The clock tower and a smaller campanile might have been copied from one of David Hockney's illustrations for the tales collected by the brothers Grimm.

Mrs Aya Kiuchi was a weaver whose entrepreneurial energies had enabled her to gather the financial resources to construct this unexpected and impressive building. No monastic references had been intended in the design, she would tell us later, but the longer we spent beneath its roof the stronger grew my impression of a religious intent on somebody's part. (I use the word "religious" in its older sense of one who has made vows which bind that person back to the Mother House.) We had arrived early and out of season, and as we stood beneath the portico I sensed that even Mr Urashima was a little awed. A lunette in stained glass was inset above the double entrance. The heavy doors of weathered copper – embossed with reliefs of a faun and a nymph – had been folded back, and through the glass panels of a pair of inner doors we could see a small, middle-aged woman in black arranging flowers in jars on a window ledge, while a much taller and much younger woman in the attitude of an acolyte stood ready to wheel to the next station a trolley loaded with jars of fresh flowers: here was the Head of House going about her everyday morning oblations. Only when she had passed into her own private apartments did we dare to step into the spacious entrance hall.

The interior was no less ecclesiastical than the exterior: on entering one instinctively lowered one's voice. This was a place where silence ruled and ritual regulated the hours. The entrance hall was floored with polished red brick, the pitched ceiling ribbed with wooden beams. Since we had arrived early, we were directed to a restaurant on the second floor. Here we saw that Mrs Kiuchi, a craftswoman herself, was also a collector of the craft of others. Their sculpted works stood on shelves and window embrasures, or waited to be transported to stand outside in the open once the snow had melted, while framed paintings stood propped against the walls. Each table and chair had been skilfully fashioned in lovely pale wood by the gifted cabinet-makers who work in Asahikawa; the seats and backs of the chairs were clothed in tapestries made here in the weaving workshop. The company's emblem was carved in deep relief on each table and chair and on the wooden menu boards, and was worn by the men in their lapels, by the women pinned to their blouses. It was the frontal bone of a ram's skull, with curled horns, the curls like eye sockets, the bone embossed with what I took at first to be a diviner's rod but was perhaps the spindle upon which the wool was to be spun. The spirit that presided over the house was Pan, the father of the flocks whose wool is the staple of the weaver's trade.

A man who was perhaps Mrs Kiuchi's secretary came up, introduced himself, and led us off. He conducted us through a sequence of rooms where, in display cases made of Hokkaido elm, the textiles that have brought renown to their creator hung attached to wooden frames. A weaver was sitting at her loom, flanked by traditional spinning wheels and demonstration carding tools, yarns of wool of varying weight laid out on tables, of a thousand different colours, said our guide. Finally, our guide led us through heavy wooden doors into the apartments of the mistress of these mysteries. It felt as if we were indeed being inducted into the presence of an abbess, the mother superior of some great religious order, as in one of the gothic tales of Isaak Dinesen. The style of the room was Germanic, and the mantelpiece was of three massive blocks of stone end to end; logs in the grate burned with a pale, incense-infused flame.

She was seated at her desk, absorbed in her calligraphy, the Japanese way of the brush, and only when she had completed a line did she carefully lay down her brush, stand, and turn towards her visitors. She was wearing black trousers, but her upper garments were folded chastely, black over white, revealing only the narrow "V" of her throat. She declined, politely but firmly, to have her photograph taken and told us that she could spare us ninety minutes. The young votary who had earlier assisted her mistress with the flowers slipped in and out of the room like a wraith, bearing dishes of tea and tiny saucers with biscuits that resembled communion wafers, each inlaid with a crystalized violet, which she placed before us on small trays, but they were much too beautiful to eat.

When, twenty-six years earlier, the Hokkaido prefectural government had approached Mrs Kiuchi to ask if she would oversee the collecting of yarn from resident flocks of sheep to stimulate the local farming economy, she was already a successful business woman. She had at the same time begun to take an interest in the traditional weaving skills of the indigenous Ainu, she told us. And though her training in the arts had been in music and painting, she had understood at once that this was the sign for which her life had prepared her. Her father had been a forester, her mother had played the koto, the traditional thirteen-stringed instrument of old Japan, and they had given her the name Aya.

One of the several meanings of the name Aya links the making of music to the craft of weaving: the strings of the warp like those of a harp, the weft the melody that the shuttle weaves. The warp may also represent the demands of an instrument, while the woof represents the individual's own gifts of performance. The signs were unmistakeable, said Mrs Kiuchi. She told us that she had chosen to call her company "Yukara Ori" because *ori* also has multiple meanings, one being "woven fabric", while in the Ainu language *yukara* can signify "hand down" or "pass on", as well as referring to the saga of the Ainu, the tale of their origins.

Although as a child she had accompanied her father around the forests of Hokkaido, Mrs Kiuchi said that in those days she had herself hardly ever met any Ainu, for at that time her principal interest had been flowers and their arrangements, and she had also been drawn to the mysteries of standing bodies of water, such as Lake Mashu, in the Akan National Park. The depths of Lake Mashu are famously unplumbed and its surface often hides behind a veil of mist, holding humans at a distance. As her understanding of the weaver's craft grew, so did her respect for the skill with which the Ainu used the fibres of plants and the bark of trees. What she learned from them later taught her how she might herself become a weaver, if there was time. For what Geoffrey Chaucer said of writing, "the lyf so short, the craft so longe to lerne" – applies to learning any craft. Your life may be over before you begin to understand it, let alone master it.

Mrs Kiuchi understood that she had first to submit herself to her loom, and that only after she had spent years studying weaving – and had for as many more years sat before her loom – would she know what to do. The craft had to come first. She strongly rejected the designation "artist" and what she saw as the pretension that the term often entails. She expressed contempt for the dilettante, and the mindlessness of the doctrine of self-expression. She was an artisan, she insisted, and what she had to do was to spend time contemplating what she sought to understand and discovering what, in her case, the loom could tell her about how to do it. This had meant up to eight years between the initial act of coming upon her subject and the completion of a piece on her loom. As she waited in front of a place such as Lake Mashu for it to reveal its genius loci, so she waited for the loom to tell her what to do with whatever she had found. The work would stand and fall by its quality as a piece of weaving, by the weaver's submissive fidelity to the medium itself.

What I wrote down, as Mr Urashima translated Mrs Kiuchi's words, was "nothing can be taken in at a glance", or reduced to a plain statement in plain words. Everything has more than two sides, the world of nature no less than the human beings who inhabit it. In her wish to understand the many expressions of Lake Mashu, Mrs Kiuchi visited it countless times, in all seasons: in autumn when the steep sides of its tree-lined inner core are multi-coloured, in winter when the only colours are white and blue. Although the surrounding temperature often falls to minus 20°C, the lake rarely freezes, and it was only when, on one of her visits, she saw the lake as it was about to freeze that she knew that this was the moment for which she had been waiting. Similarly, when she attempted to absorb the essence of *Rosa rugosa*, she spent three years looking at it before the rose spoke to her, and not until then was she able to settle down and weave. I asked if it was the flower that spoke to her or some greater power that spoke through the flower. It was the flower that spoke, she said. When I wondered why it took quite so long for her settle down to weave, she replied "the warp rejects me". She was often baffled, and might, in her excitement, lose the thread; it was always a struggle to find her way through the tangles of her loom; she had to wait, and wait again, until the loom was ready. Like so many of the craftsmen and women I met, Mrs Kiuchi spoke of this moment in terms of an epiphany.

At the beginning, she said, she had made sketches in oils, but had found that these were a hindrance rather than a help. She began to understand that however clearly or vaguely she had been seeing the design in her head, she could only translate it into a material substance when the warp accepted the propriety of the woof. Like the other craftsmen that I met, as she worked her fingers would find themselves drawn to something unforeseen but inevitable. In T. S. Eliot's phrase from *Four Quartets*, she would "know the place for the first time"; like falling in love, in James Baldwin's words, this might come as a shock, but there would be no mistake, "its truth must be borne".

You had to submit yourself to nature, said Mrs Kiuchi, you had to allow yourself to trust nature and what it gives you; you must never try to impose yourself upon her, resist her, nor dictate to her. Only by being obedient to nature can you ever hope to share your insights, or hope to move others as you yourself have been moved. Only when she had found in her loom the swan-white and cobalt blue of the ice-floes that gather in the winter off the coast of Abashiri was she able to find the way to weave them as they had asked her to weave them. So it was, too, with the white spires of the skunk cabbage in their ice-cream cones of pale green pushing up through the melting ice in boggy ground where alders cool their feet, and with the bushy *Rosa rugosa* that in June stretches for miles like beds of thrift in dunes beside the shore of the Okhotsk Sea. And with the mysterious, tree-lined caldera of Lake Mashu in autumn, when bands of yellow, crimson and bronze thread their way through the sombre ground of the darkest holly-green.

Years before I met Mrs Kiuchi, I had bought a piece of her work, or of work woven in her workshop: the warp is peacock blue, the woof mostly black, the overall effect sea-green; bands of red, copper and yellow swell or sink to a narrow wedge, or float across parts of the surface like clouds, or modulate as the changing light plays across them. Other styles made in her workshop are more abstract: on narrow vertical hangings, strata in many colours become horizons of repeated motifs, in different weights and depths of wool; sometimes a pattern like a wave may lie between parallel bands of a plain colour; sometimes a succession of small peaks may cross the warp like the recorded signals of a cardiogram; sometimes an upright shuttle recurs as a vertical motif linked by a simple thread.

Since only a few people nowadays work in such styles, and as the techniques are therefore in danger of being lost, Mrs Kiuchi saw it as her duty to act as a link in the chain by which both the technique of weaving and the work made by a weaver may be preserved. Yet as she was running a business and the artisans whom she employed had to live; what they wove was there to be used as well as enjoyed for its own sake. While she was the creator of the primary designs, thousands of facsimiles of her work have been woven by her band of assistants – such as the one that I had purchased. These can be used as furnishing fabrics, table runners or cushion covers, some even made up as cloaks and handbags; they can be found on sale in every hotel gift shop on the island, to be bought by visitors as souvenirs. However arduous and long-suffering Mrs Kiuchi's creation of the original might have been, it could, like an etching or an engraving, be reproduced as many times as you liked, her own hand hidden, yet its workings still visible.

The English translation of the name of Mrs Kiuchi's workshop was "Folk Weaving Museum" and she had recently built an annex in which she housed tapestries collected from all over the world, but she called her own working space a gallery, though it was also a workshop. The work carried out within its walls was venerable, the workers dedicated to a way of life that was, as I have suggested, in the original sense of the word, religious. In spite of Mrs Kiuchi's personal fame, her gallery had, as she may have intended, an atmosphere of anonymity, such as you find in any religious house where its members are committed to the same purpose. This was a house of relationships: between a craftswoman and the natural world, between traditional techniques and individual skills, between the maker of an object and whoever might contemplate the thing that was made, between a teacher and her students, who would carry on her work after she had died, between the past and the future, even between earth and heaven. Mrs Kiuchi was aware of the essential part that she played in binding these aspects together. She was the undoubted mistress of a major establishment, a woman of strong character and determined purpose, but she was also humble before her craft and lowly in her own eyes.

Our ninety minutes had quickly run out and the time came for us to be on our way, but as we gathered ourselves together to take our leave, Mrs Kiuchi surprised us, as Mr Kinoshita the swordmaker had surprised us. Something about the way our conversation had gone must have pleased her, for after a few whispered words with her acolyte, she invited us to stay for lunch. So, as we ate our *soba* – of buckwheat noodles – in the more relaxed atmosphere of her French Provincial dining room, I felt that I might ask why she had chosen to build in so obviously monastic a manner. She said that it was just that she loved old things and wanted a traditional building, one that might have been rooted there for centuries and was suited to the climate of Hokkaido; the fact that it looked like a monastery was accidental. I could not help thinking, though, that her architect must have known what he was doing.

In 1989, the year before we went to see her, there had been seven hundred visitors and Mrs Kiuchi believed that this was because they knew that they would be able to see at first hand that her business was not just talk. She was herself a very good talker,

and during lunch we learned more about the steel in her character that had driven her thus far in her enterprise. Her beginnings
had not been privileged by wealth or status, nor had her progress
been easy: her first efforts had been mocked by some of her com-
patriots, but when she began to win gold medals in Europe as
well as in Japan, they changed their tune. She smiled. I did not
ask whether she saw any discrepancy between one of her original
pieces of work, so long in its gestation, and the reproductions
of that work which had been woven again and again by her
associates; had I done so, I sensed she might have brushed the
question aside. She had earlier explained that she was an artisan
not an artist and had no special claim on her work, although she
took pride in her skill and her insight.

Is there a difference between the value of Mrs Kiuchi's
original work and its copies, between the authentic and the
reproductions? A clandestine copy of the Mona Lisa is consid-
ered a forgery, but the reweaving of a master design is not, and
is offered as a work of craft in its own right. The attention that
the weaver must pay to the warp of the loom and the shuttled
weft calls for attention, and will have its own authenticity. We
can recognise what has been made with love and what has not.
It struck me that Mrs Kiuchi's finished pieces could be thought
of as icons, worthy of respect as objects in and for themselves,
though Mrs Kiuchi might have rejected this suggestion. Some of
the best-known icons are those of the Pantocrator, the depiction
of Christ in the domes of Byzantine churches. These images are
indexes to the creator of the world, yet with an authority of their
own, in themselves powerful rather than pointing to a power
that has given them their power. While images of this kind are
replicable, they each remain the work of individual hands. (This
will be as true of the salmon-hunting bears of Hokkaido tourist

craft as it is of an etching by Rembrandt, or one by Yuriko Oido.) If you have a puritan view of art, icons of the Pantocrator, or images of the Virgin or Christ on the Cross, are problematic, for they can easily become objects of worship in themselves; and if you are an iconoclast, you will therefore wish to destroy them. Mrs Kiuchi's weavings are unproblematic in this sense: they do not take over God's role as the creator of a given human life, but they are as much objects of contemplation as a Persian carpet, or a wall-painting of a garden full of flowers. What gives them authority is commitment to the craft, and the way that they were hung in her gallery invited that kind of attention. Whatever emotions or feelings they arouse, these will be personal to the observer, and no one other than the viewer can claim to know what they may or may not symbolize.

The business of weaving, it is worth noting, may be even older than the fashioning of pots. The first known examples are neolithic nets and baskets woven at least seven thousand years ago, and early man, who imitates nature, may first have learned from other creatures to do with their hands what spiders do with their legs and birds do with their beaks. Spinning and weaving are primal crafts; their practitioners can trace their lineage to the very beginnings of humanity. A reader of an early version of this essay thought that I had been less impressed by Mrs Kiuchi than by the other craftsmen and craftswomen whom I had met. I was surprised, for I had been hugely impressed by her. I felt that the work produced by her and her fellow weavers was worthy of great respect, and that it was no accident that her gallery had the look of a dedicated religious house, where the intention was to achieve wholeness of eye, hand, and heart, a place where natural beauty, ancient craft and creative talent might find their affinities in an act of harmonious reconciliation.

Prabakhar Naik Satam, weaver

One April afternoon, several years before I met Mrs Kiuchi, my friend Mrs Yasuko Suginome and I caught the bus to Teine, on the way to Otaru, to visit another weaver, one trained in a different tradition. During my early years in Sapporo, Mrs Suginome had helped with great kindness to ease my passage through the novel byways of Japanese life; on this occasion she accompanied me because of her own wish to visit the weaver Prabakhar Naik Satam. Among her other voluntary activities she helped at the bookshop in Sapporo's Museum of Modern Art, and had already met Mr Naik Satam, whose vast, made-to-measure tapestry hung then in the atrium of the museum.

Unlike almost all the other craftsmen I met, Mr Naik Satam was not a *dohsanko*, a "Hokkaido horse", as people from Hokkaido call themselves. He had met his Japanese wife while they had been working in what was then Czechoslovakia, and they had sought to preserve their own identities as an Indian and a Japanese while living together in harmony. He was a man of strong views, and it was important to him that we should understand that such a condition of mutual respect was what it meant to be "international". He had chosen to live in Hokkaido, he said, because he had been told that sheep now grazed its reclaimed pastures. This was an exaggeration. I was aware that, in the 1870s, Colonel W. S. Clark, an American who became the first president of the Sapporo Agricultural College (later Hokkaido University, where I taught), had visited sheep farms in California and reported back on the prospects of sheep-farming in Hokkaido's recently colonised land, and I was delighted once, on a visit to the north of Hokkaido, to see a flock of black-faced Suffolks, but I knew that Colonel Clark's plans to develop sheep farming had been only partially satisfied.

On arrival in Hokkaido, Mr Naik Satam had been dismayed to find that he would have to seek his wool elsewhere. He spoke nostalgically of Scottish wool, and was sad that his had to come from New Zealand. (In Hokkaido it is not only wool that comes from New Zealand: one of Hokkaido's distinctive dishes, Genghis Khan, lamb sliced thin and cooked with onions and potatoes on a metal grill that resembles a Mongol helmet, is made these days with New Zealand lamb.) Farmers in Hokkaido, he said, had been looking only for immediate profit, which was, he went on, not possible in such a business; you had to wait a long time. His view was that Hokkaido was so rich in natural resources that farmers felt that they did not have to take any real trouble, which meant that they did not care enough about quality, nor were they interested in the quality of the work done by others.

He showed us his looms. He had three: the largest, which filled the wall of the room in which it stood, had been made to his own design by a local carpenter; the smallest, on which he tried out new designs, was also custom-made; he had made the third, medium-sized one himself out of odds and ends that he had found about the place when he and his wife had moved in. He had only praise for Japanese technical ability, in this and other contexts. He recognised a desire for perfection, at least of appearances, he said, but was upset by the lack of encouragement given in Japan to the free play of the creative imagination. It does not matter how tall or short a woman is, he said, how fat or thin, she is only able to buy a kimono whose uniform size must fit everyone.

While he approved of the "one village, one product" policy that was being promoted and practised by the Hokkaido government, he thought the difficulty lay not in finding a product but in getting the villagers to care about its design, and being willing to invent designs that they had never seen before. He told us that for the first nine months of his stay in Hokkaido he had lived in the village of Otoineppu, working with a group of local women. He had set up two groups: one that made silk-screen designs while the other wove them, and he still visited the group each month. He was pleased with the exhibition that his group put on at the end of their nine months together. He was not interested in turning out pupils who copied somebody else's designs. It disturbed him, he said, that many of his Japanese friends did not appear to care about thinking for themselves. He blamed the *tonden* spirit for this, though not the *tonden-hei* themselves: he understood that the government had given the settlers a job to do, but there was no tradition of aesthetic appreciation upon which their descendants could draw.

He told us, as he continued in this critical strain, that he had noted an obsession with money, the desire for a quick return. Although no one would deny that one needed money to live, he said, this ought not to be in our minds when we are at work. If the work is good, people will buy it, if we wait. The people of Hokkaido were not prepared to wait, or so he believed; they thought of their work only in terms of how quickly they could sell it. It was why they had given up keeping sheep. He believed, he added, that respect for authority was a major problem. The teacher has absolute authority, often unwarranted. He did not want his students to think of him as *sensei*, the teacher who must be obeyed. If we are asked to explain our work it takes away any joy that we may have felt in its creation. We must reawaken the sense of pleasure that we feel when we work with our hands.

Naik Satam's own works exemplify his views, for they are like no one else's, either in scale or design. There are influences, however: the immense tapestry of his hanging in the Sapporo Museum of Modern Art appears to take motifs from cubism and tantra, often explicitly sexual. He had learned his craft in France, he said. It had been at the Gobelins tapestry factory on the out-skirts of Paris that he discovered ways to express his sense of his Indian heritage of Buddhist beliefs and Tantric iconography. (Whether those who wove the royal tapestries in the Gobelins and Aubusson workshops would acknowledge his handiwork as part of their own heritage, who can say – but they might have enjoyed its inventiveness.) As soon as the people of India have ideas, said Mr Naik Satam, they "bang them away to other people", but, he added, the people of Japan are not able to do this, not because they lack generosity, for as hosts they are wonderfully generous, but because in public they shield themselves from other's eyes; they hate to stand out, unless they are public performers, who enjoy playing the fool.

What my companion Mrs Suginome made of Mr Naik Satam's views of Japanese character I did not ask: she would have heard it all before. Somebody had told Naik Satam that many Japanese believe that if you give anything of yourself, then you lose what-ever it is that you have given, and can never recover it. He, on the contrary, said he believed that the more you give, the more you are truly yourself. He had heard, he told us, of a Japanese teacher of the Japanese language who had argued that when you are talking to foreigners, you lose your Japanese identity; again, he thought that the opposite was true: he believed that as you seek to explain your culture to a foreign visitor, you will be far more likely to discover what your own true identity is. He wanted his Japanese co-workers to recover a sense that modern man had lost: a sense of the person himself as part of a whole-ness of which every part is deserving of respect, extending those relationships to embrace the members of other nations.

Not long after I met him, Mr Naik Satam and his wife moved to Nagoya, in the middle of Honshu, where Honshu takes its sharp turn to the west, and not long after he settled there he completed three pieces for a gallery in Yokohama, a city half way between Nagoya and Tokyo. He had told us that he was beginning to feel old and that these would be his last works. I wondered if he would really abandon his looms, or whether he had just decided to move on again, in order to find more in himself that he still wanted to give.

I, too, am old, but I have not yet closed the gate on a final-ly-harvested field, and back and forth I go to collect left-over sheaves. Although Samuel Johnson said that you should always delete anything that you are particularly pleased with, I will indulge myself here with some further reflections on migration, and the weaving and spinning of language.

I do not myself care to be asked why I left my homeland – I miss it, though I am grateful to be where I am – so I did not ask Mr Naik Satam why he had left his. As a weaver he belonged to a guild with a long history, and he may have needed a wider space within which to work. Exiles who have a trade cannot help but become international, and whether they go wandering by choice or by chance, their skills are often welcomed by those amongst whom they find themselves beached. When you cross physical boundaries, you bear gifts, those that you fashion with your hands when you get there, or those that you carry in your knapsack. These are gifts of the spirit, and overstep boundaries.

Our unhappy world is full of migrants, forced from their homes, but they, too, bring gifts. Migrant weavers epitomise this. We can find an example in Europe. Louis XIV's persecution of Protestants in France and the Low Countries led to the diaspora of weavers, from France the Huguenots, from the Low Countries members of the Reformed Churches. Yet Louis allowed them to take their looms and their skills, with them. We may imagine them pausing to look back at the bank of a canal – maybe high with recent rain – at old houses reflected in the water beneath a pink-flushed evening sky, at the diminishing spires of the city where they had been born, or, moving south, pausing in a Burgundian vineyard with the sun setting over the homeland that they were leaving. Many Huguenot weavers chose to come to Britain and settled in London, in Spitalfields. Here they passed on their skills to those who made a place for them, as did later refugees, with other skills, those who fled from Nazi Germany or Communist Russia. Those who are peregrine – to use T.S.Eliot's term again – by their own choice, rather than being displaced by flood, fire or the horrors of war, may be most welcomed by those amongst whom they settle. In my own experience, if you settle among the Japanese you are particularly fortunate, for the Japanese are wonderfully hospitable to everyone who has gifts that they wish to make use of, and they are grateful for whatever you may have it in you to give.

The words that we use in English for spinning and weaving and how these relate to other crafts are also worth a moment's thought. The users of Early English took over from their Anglo-Saxon forebears words such as "worth", "world", "wood" and "wool", as they also took over the words "web" and "weave", "warp" and "woof". In Anglo-Saxon, "loom" was the word for a tool – for any tool. A loom was a weaver's most important tool and the word "tool" came to denote any and every kind of implement that men used when fashioning the things that they made. (Etymologists tell us that "tool" was derived from "taw", which meant to prepare something, anything, for use.) Such word-histories illustrate the role of metonymy in the development and diversity of the English tongue.

So, too, with spinning and weaving, a complex process: the spinner takes wool from the sheep, or silk from the silkworm, or the hair of a plant of the hollyhock family, then twists these strands of wool, or silk or flax into yarn. Spinning is a primal craft, prior even to weaving. The spinner's key instrument is a distaff, a small stick or shaft, upon which a dise, of wool or flax, is wound before the spinner draws it from the spindle in a thread suitable for weaving. This was originally women's work, the "distaff side" of the family's tasks. It is a division of labour that is written into the folktales of Northern Europe, where a girl sits by the fire while she waits for the stranger who will bring the golden thread that she needs to spin out her days, or where, in another part of the shadow-filled mediæval forest, a princess pricks her finger on a spindle, and sleeps for a hundred years, until, centuries later, as the story is told by Tchaikovsky and Marius Petipa in their ballet *The Sleeping Beauty*, she is woken by Prince Florimund. For as long as the ballet continues to be staged, she will continue to be thus magically restored to life

When the yarn has been prepared, it is stretched from top to bottom of the loom: this is the warp, a word that once meant "throw" but can also mean, if it refers to wood, "shrink", or, if the wind winds through it, "moan". The weaver takes other strands of yarn and weaves them in and out of the stretched-out yarn of the warp using a shuttle: this is the weft, or woof, both from the verb "to weave", while from the Latin verb for weave, *textere*. we derive a range of other English terms for this and other crafts: textile, texture, and text. A writer, for example, weaves words to create a text, which may have a certain texture, rough or smooth, plain or elaborate; he or she can also spin a yarn.

In Greek a builder was called *tekton*, from which "technique", "technical" and "technology" are derived. The root word *techne* meant "art", "craft" or "skill", which suggests that the Greeks did not make the distinction that we do between these branches of human handiwork, that they did not worry about questions such as "what is art?" or "what is craft?". For the Greeks, what was well-made was *teknikos*, well-crafted – in English, though, "crafty" has taken on more sinister associations, perhaps because crafts were mysteries, and their secrets were kept close to the chest.

Even today, in the remotest parts of Europe, on Hebridean islands and in secluded Welsh valleys, weavers – mostly women – weave garments by choice; they know that machines can do the work more economically, but those who weave in the old way do not believe that machines are as efficient or the results so pleasing. Thus the oldest of all handcrafts survives, in enclaves, in stories, and inscribed in language itself.

Norio Tokita, poet

I n late August 1990, I stood at the head of the Nissho Pass, looking eastward over the Tokachi Plain with the party of visiting soil scientists that we met earlier. I gazed with them at the pastures and tillage on the plain below, features of the landscape that were undoubtedly new. One of the visitors expressed surprise that after only a hundred years under the plough, the prospect should remind him of an Italian landscape that had been farmed for centuries. Another observed that it reminded her of Provence, and thought it remarkable that what appeared to be an ageless mosaic of field and furrow had been until only recently primeval forest. Looking out over the plain, we could begin to make out in the morning haze the mountains that bounded the neatly-ordered patchwork landscape: the stubble of wheat fields recently reaped, leafy beet ready to be pulled, squares of dark volcanic soil ploughed and waiting to be sown again, stitched together by ranks of larch and silver birch. I knew by then that living and working on the plain below were farmers who had at least as deep an understanding of the land as the soil scientists had – and a deeper understanding than Mr Naik Satam had given them credit for when he rebuked them for their impatience, since among them lived farmers for whom the land was not only a matter of making a living: some of them, I had learned, were also poets.

One morning earlier that year, Mr Urashima had driven me to visit such a poet-farmer, one who worked his fields by day and after supper retired upstairs to his book-filled room to write poetry. Traces of snow still lingered on the Tokachi plain as we drove towards Norio's farm, but spring comes to Tokachi earlier than to other parts of Hokkaido, and as we entered the gate we had to swing around a shrubbery of azaleas already in flower, as if it had been a suburban garden in Britain. An old man was weeding the shrubbery; a sheep-dog barked wildly, almost strangling itself on its chain. The farmhouse, which looked south-west towards the Hidaka mountain range, was new, and we sat in a carpeted room from which, through plate-glass windows, we could see the old man at work in the garden. The room had an air of Sunday afternoon repose that reminded me of well-to-do farm parlours that I had known in the rural borderland that runs between England and Wales. It was not at all typical of other Hokkaido farmhouses that I visited. In our conversation with Mr Tokita Mr Urashima suggested that its comfort indicated unusual financial success. Mr Tokita replied, sharply, that he worked very hard.

Mr Tokita was a farmer because his father, who was the old man in the garden, had been a farmer before him; his grandfather, too, had been a farmer, but not by birth. Like some of the early colonists who had moved up from Niigata he had settled in Otaru as a merchant, then in the year Meiji 30 (1897) he had moved to Obihiro, where he began a new life as a banker. He had been too honest, said his grandson, and the bank had lost its way. Only then did he try his hand at farming, although after some initial success that too had failed. It was his grandfather's failure rather than his father's later success that challenged Mr Tokita: he farmed and wrote to wipe out the pain of defeat.

Mr Urashima translated these words as "to challenge his grandfather". What Mr Tokita meant, it became clear, was that the example set by what he called his grandfather's "dauntless heart" in the face of his tribulations was a gage thrown down that his grandson had had to pick up. His grandfather had been recruited for his mercantile skills – he had not been one of the original settlers, the *tonden-hei*, but he had shown the true *tonden* spirit, one that his grandson wished to emulate by accepting as a challenge the demands of the farming life, especially farming on a large scale. His grandfather's life was his model, his grand-father's purpose his purpose; and where his grandfather had failed, he would succeed, as if he meant to compensate his grandfather for the old man's misfortunes by setting them in reverse, and thus reconcile his ancestor's spirit to its loss.

The writing of verse sets up its own challenges, and Mr Tokita had responded to them to wide acclaim. He writes *tanka*, the five-line, thirty-one syllable verses that are also sometimes called *waka*. It is a more venerable form than its better-known offshoot, *haiku*, and no less revered. Hokkaido supports many branches of a Tokyo-based society of poets who compose *tanka*; they correspond with each other and take part in competitions; the Empress hosts an annual reading of *tanka* at the Imperial Palace. As the *tanka* form challenges the poet, so the poems that Mr Tokita writes challenge, quite purposefully, a number of conventionally-held opinions: most notably, that if you mean to create a true work of art the wilds of Hokkaido are not the place to do so. He wished to contest the metropolitan view of the farmer as an uncouth man with dirty fingernails, too bowed down by the hardships of his life to appreciate, let alone to create, a work of art.

It was understandable that he did not appear to be especially pleased with a photograph of himself that had just been published in a book of portraits of distinguished Hokkaido artists, *Northern Features*, by the photographer Masahide Sato. He had the book and showed us the picture: in black and white, he stands against a background of his own fields; his longish hair is swept back into the fur collar of his windcheater; half an inch of ash protrudes from the cigarette held loosely between his lips. The picture needs no colour to suggest that his weather-beaten face is darkly tanned, with something of the rusticity of Ms Oido's round-faced ladies, more the farmer than the poet. It did not look at all like the still-youthful face of the man who was sitting opposite me.

Mr Tokita had first come across collections of *tanka* in the school library of his primary school. Even at that age, he thought that he could do as well as the poets in print, and by doing so to oppose the view that the farmer's life is dark and dismal. Since *tanka* is such a highly-esteemed form, it seemed the ideal means to take on those he thought of as ignorant poseurs in their Tokyo ivory towers. He rejected no less vigorously the opposite, equally sentimental view of country life that P. G. Wodehouse, the British author and humourist, spoke of as "apple-cheeked villagers and honeysuckle round the door". As a teacher of literature at the Farmers' College in Honbetsu, he had a duty, he felt, to encourage his fellow farmers to have faith in their way of life, to believe that it was a healthy and honest career, that their lives were fully human. He had the same message for those in cities: to work in close touch with the earth benefits those who do so as well as those who enjoy the fruits of their work.

Mr Tokita joined the local branch of the national *tanka* society, and a national magazine published one of his poems while he was still at school. When I asked, he confirmed my understanding that in Japanese society membership of a group of workers in the same field is essential to your personal well-being, strengthening your sense of commitment to that work and your own performance. Mr Tokita's first model was the leader of the group that he had joined twenty-five years earlier, Fumiko Nakaju. As she had done, he found it useful to talk things over with members of the group, a collaborative rather than competitive community. For all the Japanese suspicion of individualism and its temptations, however, excellence is still recognised. No less than victory in the games of Go that are televised each Sunday, the writing of award-winning *tanka* is of national interest, and people follow it as keenly as they do the performance of their local sumo wrestling hero. When Mr Tokita's first book of *tanka* was published, ten years before we met him, he became, like Lord Byron, famous overnight. He was awarded Japan's highest prize for poetry, the Gendai Kajin Association Award. No one living in Hokkaido had ever received the award before, and metropolitan publishers were eager to publish his collections: a fifth volume of his poems was due to be published the following autumn, and a selection of his work was about to appear that June in an anthology of *tanka* from Basho onwards. Mr Tokita did not appear to be in the least abashed by the company he was now keeping.

One of my own preoccupations as a performer and pedagogue is rhythm, but the rhythmic characters of the English and Japanese languages are seas apart. All spoken languages are more or less isochronic: they move, that is, to a regularly-timed beat, but Japanese is syllable-timed, each syllable falling on the beat, while English is stress-timed, the beat falling on the syllable that takes the stress. This is the feature of English speech that the Japanese find hardest to hear and most difficult to imitate, and why, conversely, it is not sensible to think that one can write *tanka* in English just by adhering to the number of syllables set out in the same five-line pattern. It is even more difficult should you try to write a three-line *haiku*.

While English verse has come these days to rely for its energy and vitality on a dynamic rhythm rather than a fixed metre, the often flaccid jottings that pass for *tanka* in English reveal the unsuitability of the form: it is over before it has started, if it has not fallen flat on its face. Those who write *tanka* in English do not agree, because they would like us to believe that the writer's subjective feelings are what matter most, whereas what matters most – not only in *tanka* but in every other kind of verse in whatever language that verse is written – must be the concordant association of sounds in a congenial and rhythmic dance of words that may or may not be metrical: without such harmony, you will not have a poem, however interesting or important your ideas or feelings may be.

I have found when writing up an interview that it may be all too easy to ask your interviewee if he or she agrees with some opinion of your own and then, as it were, to put the words you are seeking into their mouths, but in Mt Tokita's case he really did seem to have similar views to mine. I told him that I had read that more than a million people in countries around the world were writing *tanka* in English and that I thought this a misguided enterprise, since you need time to establish a rhythm in English whereas in Japanese it is already given you before you begin. When Mr Urashima translated my remarks into Japanese, Mr Tokita seemed eager to agree. And when I said that T. S. Eliot had remarked that when he had a problem with a poem, it was always of a musical nature, Mr Tokita, who had not heard of Eliot, agreed with that, too.

He said that the meanings of the words he used were not as important in producing the effect he wished to convey as the sounds: bright, clear sounds in a happy rhythmic relationship, which would create the particular cry that he was anxious to set echoing in the listener's ear. He spoke of his strong rejection of what Mr Urashima translated as a "slave rhythm". I was puzzled by the phrase, but it became clear that he meant not so much a rhythm as a recurrent dark image, that cosmopolitan writers call up in composing poems about the farmer's life. To illustrate, by contrast, the bright sounds that he meant to create Mr Tokita read aloud a *tanka* that he had written; he read it through several times. It consisted only of the syllable *pa*, repeated to the set ordering of the rhythmic units in the proper alignments that the *tanka* form prescribes; it reminded me of Papageno and Papagena's joyful duet as they recognise each other at the end of Mozart's *The Magic Flute*.

Mr Tokita had also taken on the job of selecting the best among the several hundred poems submitted by farmer poets every other month to a farming magazine called Iehnohikari. I asked him what qualities he looked for in the poems that he selected. He often chose poems about trees, he told me, and what he looked for in such verses was that they should be warm. I already knew that he had a practical relation to trees as director of the Tokachi Forestry Association, and I asked him what this work entailed. The association is similar to an agricultural cooperative, and his job was to oversee the management of the mountain woodlands, to arrange for the sale of plots of forest, and find work for its members. He had himself recently bought twenty-five hectares of forest in the foothills of the Hidaka mountain range. When I asked him if, like me, he sometimes touched his trees affectionately, or talked to them, he said that he thought of them as his friends and colleagues. He loved them as much when they were in leaf, he said, as when their branches were bare.

I asked if he was hopeful about the future of the forests. He did not answer directly, but said that as a result of foreign criticism of Japanese overseas logging practices, Japan had to reconsider the use and management of its own resources, that more trees would have to be felled, and that Japan would consequently have to reconsider its consumption of paper as well as ensuring better coordination between the several agencies that were active in the forestry business. As the logging companies were felling but not replanting, the government had to encourage more tree-planting days. These were now becoming popular, he said, Emperor Akihito setting an example.

I wondered how Mr Tokita balanced his various tasks. Did he compose poems while at work on the farm? No, never. On the farm, he concentrated on his tractor, and as he was not thinking of his poems, he was storing energy for them, the energy on which he would draw when every evening after supper he went up to his study, void of furniture bar bookcases and a low table at which he sat on the floor. He invited us to see it, and Mr Urashima took a photograph of him at his table, with his papers, brushes and pens. In the photograph Mr Tokita wears a black, V-necked sweater with short sleeves, and his bare forearms are placed squarely on the table. His long hair merges with the background shadow cast by the flash of the camera, at which he looks almost sternly, neither a bucolic farmer nor a city versifier, but a man of determination who knows his own mind.

When he settled down to write, I asked, what came first? Was it the words, or was it an idea he needed to express? Words always came first, he replied. And before the words was a pattern of sounds, which adjusted themselves to the particular pattern of the *tanka* rhythm. The professor of music at the old Sapporo College of Education once told me the *tanka* rhythm was not unlike the monosyllabic rhythm with which Beethoven begins his setting of Schiller's "Ode to Joy", which is why the Japanese find it so comfortable to sing, which choirs do in their thousands every Christmas, in German and without scores: they know it by heart. We went back downstairs, where Mrs Tokita had made fresh tea. Yes, he said when we asked, he was beginning to feel that he would have liked a little more personal freedom. His wife thought that he would find it: his motto, she told us, was "What I declare, that I will do."

Since Mr Tokita's poems were the only works I wrote about for Northern Lights that I was not able to appreciate at first-hand, I asked my colleague Hiroshi Watanabe when I returned to Sapporo if he could give me an idea of their quality. He told me that Mr Tokita's poems are straightforward and engaging, but that Mr Tokita would not be as widely recognised as he is if the assessment depended on what the poems say when they are paraphrased in Japanese or translated into English, for the idea that a farmer's life is not dull and gloomy but active and healthy can hardly be thought a novel or an uncommon opinion. Professor Watanabe translated a handful of Mr Tokita's *tanka* for me, and I have attempted to turn three of them into rhythmic rather than syllabic verse, but what the translations cannot convey are the very qualities that give the poems their characteristic life:

The eyes that challenge
The wilderness, they told me,
Resemble a leopard's eyes:

I have never seen a leopard, though,
Apart from the one in his cage.

The word "challenge" must continue to mean a good deal to
Mr Tokita, and Professor Watanabe told me that the poems con-
sistently challenged urbanity; they also challenged the spirit of
defeatism with which urbanity scornfully saddles the farmer.
When there was complete fusion of words and feelings, said Professor Watanabe, as in Mr Tokita's poems about his grandfather,
his wife and his children, what might strike an urbane sophis-
ticate as crudity is vividly effective. Mr Tokita also praises the
earth, the solitary tree, the lonely rock, the snow-covered fields.
He beatifies them, said Professor Watanabe, in their strength;
he blesses the ordinary and the everyday. In this respect Norio
Tokita is like the poet George Herbert, who found benediction in
the simple sweeping of a room, or the painter Chardin, who could
beatify a teapot or a jar of olives. In one of his poems, Mr Tokita
writes that he prefers his own strong neck to the slender legs to
be seen on the streets of Tokyo:

As when we see wrestlers
Dash their bodies one against
The other: he who struggles
On the frozen field has no way
Other than to stand by himself.

Or in another:

The conclusion of my debate
With the veterinarian
About northern affairs:
The tree must stand
Aloof, and aloft.

When the Tokyo critics first read such verses, they were apparently shocked by their directness and force. It says something for their disinterested love of poetry that within two years of the poems first appearing these masters of the genre awarded him the highest prize that it was in their power to give.

Mr Tokita had not read any of the poems of Robert Frost, he did not know Frost's "Two Tramps in Mud Time", but Frost, too, was both a poet and a farmer, a man who liked to chop his own wood rather than ask someone else to do it for him. When two tramps appear out of the woods and watch him cutting logs, he senses that they resent his doing what they feel is their job, and feel that Frost is denying them their rightful income by doing the work for himself. Frost, however, wishes to harmonize his two pursuits, which he calls his "avocation" and his "vocation", to create a unity between his work as a poet and his life as a farmer. He has no intention of splitting them apart:

> But yield who will to their separation,
> My object in living is to unite
> My avocation and my vocation
> As my two eyes make one in sight.
> Only when love and need are one,
> And the work is play for mortal stakes,
> Is the deed ever really done
> For Heaven and the future's sakes.

Norio Tokita seems to have succeeded in achieving Frost's ideal: he has both a vocation and an avocation, the working play of the plough and the playful work of the scrivener's brush. From his study that day we could look north out over his dun-brown fields, waiting to be planted with beans. There was a boundary hedge of silver birch running away on one side, larch on the other, off towards a horizon as flat as East Anglia. Before we left he took us for a walk so that we might smell the awakening earth. We turned to look west across a field of winter wheat and plots of sugar beet transplanted just the week before. Only twenty-five kilometres away, the ragged peaks of the Hidaka Mountain Range rose up sharp and clear as if they had been the Himalayas.

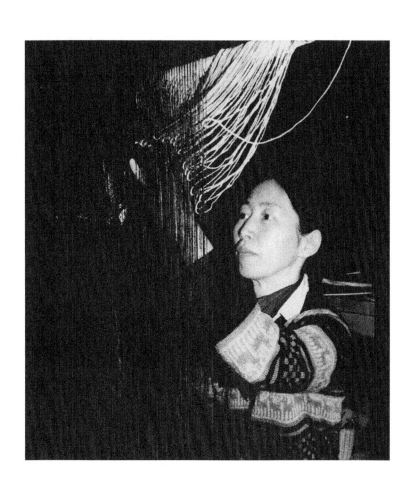

Hisako Sumi, *weaver*

I was due to meet Mr Urashima on a public holiday in late November, and for a week I wondered whether to telephone him to say that I was tired and would rather stay at home and read. But I am nervous of the telephone and fear to interrupt friends when they may be busy, and I knew that had I tried to wriggle out of it, Mr Urashima would simply have brushed my anxieties aside. So I took the train to Chitose, where Mr Urashima was to meet me. We were due to visit another weaver, one who wove into fabrics of assorted weights and lengths the hemp that her husband had dyed in vats of indigo. I shall always be grateful that on that day I did not stay at home.

Once again, Mr Urashima was not sure how to reach our destination, only that it was in the open air and that one had to climb a little way to reach it. The taxi driver was not sure, either. He took us from the air terminal to the only area of higher ground nearby – not high enough to notice if you were not looking out for it – and dropped us off at a brand-new public library, in shiny red brick, with a glazed barrel-roof over the broad central hall. One of the assistant librarians understood what we were looking for and pointed out the way to the local shrine. Here we would find our quarry on the far side of a glade, in a grove of slender *Quercus dentata*. The clouds were weeping as we scuffled through the sodden leaves, while moisture congealed in the tree-tops. It was the sort of November day that I have loved since I was a child, the woods mysterious but without menace. Two men in labourer's clothing watched us as we approached over the grass towards the shrine and what I would have called a wigwam, but was told was correctly referred to as a tepee. One of the men, with a small pigtail, a neatly trimmed moustache and a warm smile, came up to greet us.

Our host was Toshinori Sumi; his friend was the son of the assistant priest of the shrine. We introduced ourselves, and Mr Sumi invited us to enter the tent, where his wife, Hisako, was squatting on a tatami mat in front of an iron stove. Hisako was a weaver; her husband dyed the fibres that she wove. Toshinori Sumi wore heavy plastic gloves to stir the cauldrons of indigo in which he steeped the inner bark of the ramie plant, a flax-like fibre from the Malaysian peninsula that is so tough and wiry that it is practically immortal. Once it had been dyed, Hisako would weave it into abstract hangings or the mysterious shapes displayed on the grass outside the shrine like immense blocks of lapis lazuli.

Indigo is a fast dye: it does not fade in sunlight, nor lose its colour however many times you wash it. The more often you dip your material in the vat and allow the dye to oxygenate, the darker will be the blue, the richer its shade. The Japanese call indigo *ai*, but as *ai* is a homonym for "love", a word that must be used with circumspection, a pun may be dangerous, and the word should not be bandied about. A millennium and a half ago, during the Nara Era, a strict code regulated the production of indigo, and only the nobility could wear indigo-dyed clothes.

Of the methods that over time the Japanese have used to produce *ai*, the most common is known as *sukumo*. Once the leaves are dry, water is sprinkled over them and they are allowed to ferment; they are then beaten into a paste called *aidama*; the paste is mixed with lime to control the fermentation, with starch to feed the bacteria, and with water to thin it; wood-ash liquor is added later, along with more lime. The Kodansha Encyclopaedia says that this takes a week, but the Sumis said that it took them only three days. The earliest extant piece of Japanese indigo-dyed cloth dates from the seventh century, but far earlier than this people had dyed cloth in indigo: the Egyptians had a use for it, as did as did Genghis Khan and the aristocrats of imperial Rome; my Silurian ancestors boiled it down from the plant now named *Isatis tinctoria*: they called it woad.

Before the early years of the twentieth century indigo could only be made from the leaves of the plants *Indigofera* and *Isatis*, and much of the world's supply came from India, where, in 1897, nearly two million acres were devoted to its cultivation and the sub-continent exported seventeen million pounds of indigo a year. Towards the end of the nineteenth century, when German-made synthetic indigo came on the market, it contributed to a virtual collapse of the Indian economy. In Japan, too, traditional methods of producing indigo were partly abandoned, but not entirely, for 148 traditional Japanese dye-houses are apparently still active, mostly in the traditional home of *aidama*, Tokushima Prefecture in the southern island of Shikoku. Some, though, can be found in Date, a small town on the line from Sapporo to Hakodate, which was where Hisako Sumi got hers from, and maybe still does.

A few of the early settlers to Hokkaido brought *Indigofera* with them from Tokushima and attempted to grow it on land to the north of Sapporo, near the sea. Although no *Indigofera* grows there today, a newly-built township has been named Ainosato – "the heart of *ai*" – a name that ought to keep the memory of their efforts alive. Several of Hisako's pieces now hang there in one of the new apartment blocks.

The year before we met them, the Sumis had held an exhibition in Paris, where they learned that they were not alone in choosing the traditional manner of preparing indigo for traditional purposes: in Angers and Basle, they found, church fabrics were still being repaired with Japanese *aidama*; the mayor of Nancy invited the Sumis to visit his town the following year to demonstrate the virtues of authentic indigo.

In their tepee at the shrine a chimney projected through the poles at the apex, and while Toshinori fed scented wood into the small iron stove, Hisako told Mr Urashima their story. She had been inspired, as Mr Nagao had been, by a television programme: in her case, one about Swedish craftsmen who worked with indigo. She had then read an article about an anthropologist who had won an award for his fieldwork with the Ainu. No Ainu needed a course to understand how to make *ai*, the anthropologist said, or how to dye the fabrics that they wore every day.

On leaving school Hisako joined a magazine company, but stayed for only a month. A month's salary was enough to pay for one *hyo* – sixty kilos – of *ai*. She bought her first *hyo*, and took herself off to Hiroshima in order to learn the craft, as a number of dyers were still working there, but the dyers were uncooperative. Discouraged, she returned to Hokkaido and settled in Naganuma, a village not far from Chitose. Once there, she began to search Hokkaido for as yet undiscovered varieties of *Indigofera* that would yield a different blue, one that would reflect the paler skies not only of Hokkaido but of Sakhalin, Finland and Lapland, the homelands of other northern peoples related to the Ainu, the Inuit, and the Itelmen. She had still not found what she was looking for, but was determined to go on searching.

Some of those who had visited their exhibition in Paris the year before had been disappointed not to see Toshinori stirring a vat of *ai*, but everybody had been fascinated to see how Hisako created her sculptures with the dyed and woven yarns that they had taken with them. Most of her constructions are bulky, and she had had to make the pieces for the Paris show at the site itself. In Europe she had learned that, although fabrics dyed in Indian indigo can be found in Germany and London, they can be seen only in museums, and many Parisians had been intrigued enough to go to the exhibition and see her newly-woven indigo fabrics for themselves. In a poem translated into French and printed on the leaflet for Hisako's Paris show, she writes of how, on fine days in the summer, she would move her loom into the open fields. Here is my English version, based on Professor Watanabe's translation from Japanese:

> *I listen to the sound of the wind*
> *And I am in touch*
> *With the souls of living things:*
> *Water flows, living creatures breathe, time passes*
> *Slowly – but without end.*

In the tent in Chitose, with the rain beating an occasional tattoo upon the canvas covering of the tepee, we might have forgotten the passing of time, but any such illusion was broken by the roar of jet airliners taking off, close enough to drown our words, while the stove began to generate so powerful a heat that I feared my trousers might catch fire. The first visitors of the day had begun to wander over the wet grass and were anxious to speak to

Hisako about her sculptures, so I took the opportunity to follow Mr Urashima, who had gone to join Toshinori in the open air. We stood beneath my umbrella, and Toshinori told us more about his wife's creations, which, though they look monolithic, are weightless, being built of indigo-dyed fabric drawn tautly over a frame of slatted bamboo. There were two pieces laid out on the grass. The smaller of them was roughly box-shaped, the fabric in which the cube was wrapped dyed to different depths of blue, the other was an angular bolster, slightly twisted, the differing blues marking off each bevelled face as if shaved by a carpenter's plane. While I held my umbrella aloft, Toshinori lifted a flap at one end of the bolster and invited Mr Urashima to crawl inside, which he did, taking his camera with him. When it was my turn, I handed my umbrella over, but was not able to crawl in even half so far. The filtered light was a bleached aquamarine and coils of ramie lay on the ground like fisherman's tackle at the bottom of a boat, or in a mermaid's cavern beneath the sea. When I crawled out backwards and stood again, a sunbeam had for a moment made its way through the low cloud, leaving a smear of blue sky in its wake, gilding the golden strap-work on the roof timbers of the shrine.

As we stood in the rain, an old friend of Mr Urashima's, Mr Matsumoto, drove up to take us in his rather sporty little car to the Sumis' solitary farmhouse to see Hisako's loom and Toshinori's vats. Hisako squeezed into the back of the car with Mr Urashima, while I, with my awkwardly long legs, was invited to sit in the front. It was still raining and the clouds were low as we drove through water-logged farmland. We took a short-cut down an unsurfaced forest road, and I wondered if the springs of the car would stand up to the kind of rally-car driving that Mr Matsumoto seemed to be enjoying. I had by now lost all sense of direction, but just before we reached Naganuma, which lies to the north of Chitose, where fields had recently been scooped from the low swellings of the surrounding woodland, we turned sharply right into a narrow valley, where a small farmhouse and an even smaller Dutch barn were tucked, across a brook, behind a wood-break of closely-planted larch. Two dogs were tethered near the front door on a slight mound at the foot of a group of straggly pines. The larger of the dogs, who looked rather like a wolf, regarded me steadily. For all his size, Hisako told me later, as we were leaving, he was only six months old, still a puppy. His companion, a sheepdog, turned his head away. Neither of the dogs had anything to say.

The farmhouse was old and not as upholstered as Mr Tokita's; indeed it was hardly upholstered at all. It faced a field that had recently been levelled to make it easier for the plough, but after a hundred yards swept upwards like a wave about to break against the low wooded horizon, a wash of vividly-green winter wheat. A track of soft black ash led off north through the field towards a grove of leafless, rain-darkened trees that lifted their heads out of a hollow where a brook had dug a deep channel. In the summer, Hisako explained, Toshinori's vats of indigo would stand beside the stream. When, in the spring and summer, Hisako worked outside, as she wrote in the leaflet of her Paris show, her studio was the sweep of the green field, and her music the wind moving through the trees or the wheat, which would be standing as high as her elder son's head. These, for much of the day, would be the only sounds she would hear.

In the winter, though, she had to work indoors. One half of the living space was a sitting area with a stove, a low table and a settee below a range of photographs pinned to the wall. The kitchen was attached to the western side of this part of the living area, with a view of the road at the top of the bank; an abandoned conservatory opened off at the side, filled not with plants, but with the odds and ends of a busy craftswoman's life. The other half of the main living space was an eight-tatami area, not so large, most of which was taken up with a table scattered with sketches that had been drawn by her two small sons, who had arrived at the tepee as we were leaving to help their father entertain visitors. Two large screens of frosted glass opened on to a small glassed-in porch, and here, in front of the screens, Hisako had placed her loom, so that while she was working, and if it was warm enough for her to slide the windows aside, she would be able to look through the warp and weft of her work towards the snowy fields. Here she sought to learn how best to weave the dyed hanks of the ramie through the warp of her loom, attending to what the loom would permit her to do with them. She had no more interest than Mrs Kiuchi or Mr Nagao had in imposing a previously-thought-out design: the ramie, which for all its apparent fragility is more durable than metal and unaffected by heat, would reveal what it was capable of becoming.

Yet what Hisako really wanted us to understand was the part that her husband played in her work. She believed that what he contributed grew more important every day, even though, she acknowledged, had he not married her, he would have taken no interest in such work. They had been classmates in junior high school, then had met again at a gallery in Sapporo fifteen years later. He was thirty, held no position and had no particular philosophy, but she felt, she told us, that he had an unassailable innocence, that he was waiting for a sign which would direct him to something that would fill the vacancies of his life. One of his strengths was calmness of mind. She had noticed while they were in Paris how imperturbable he was, and how much this had helped her to relax; he was also single-minded, and this had helped her to persevere when she had doubted her ability and strength. After they married, she had stopped working for a while. It was Toshinori who, after six months, had said "Let us begin again". Although he had had no special training and had not felt any aptitude for working at a craft, he had taken happily to his new role. He went regularly to the Hokkaido Industrial Experimental Station on the Hokkaido University campus, where he was learning how to fashion glass and apply lacquer; he also leased a furnace at Nopporo, a primeval forest to the east of Sapporo, where he fired the glass that he had worked on. He was learning to weave and had made some textiles of his own. When he had married Hisako, he had married her work as well; he seemed entirely happy to accept its disciplines.

The conversation became desultory and I asked our hostess, while she was making coffee, if I might go for a walk. I had been drawn to the dark trees in their hollow, their crowns deep purple and rich russet with the buds of the following spring, swollen like a bruise against the dark, low clouds; the barks of spruce beside the track were mottled pale green and silver, spotted with bronze. I took my umbrella, and the wolfdog watched me as I wandered off, slightly uphill. The trees near the bank of the stream were again slender *Quercus dentata*, and as I stood at the lip of the bank looking down at the creek, the trees motionless, the only sound the pattering of rain on the woodland floor, it might have been a brook hidden in a cleft of unkempt woodland in a forgotten upland corner of the Welsh Border of my childhood. The atmosphere was entirely benign.

The wolfdog watched me as I returned, but said nothing to warn his mistress, who, when I entered the house, was squatting drinking coffee at the low table and chatting with Mr Urashima and Mr Matsumoto. I sat on the sofa and asked a few more questions, mostly about her looms. She had two, which she had put together herself. The bigger one, 1.8 metres long by 1.3 metres high, was the loom in place, and she had just completed ten large pieces of tapestry on it, for which she used ramie of various weights of yarn and assorted shades of blue.

Again, she wanted to talk about her husband. She explained that though she might have helped him find what he was capable of making of his life and what latent powers he had, he had likewise helped her to grow and understand what she was capable of. Most particularly, he had helped her to see how best to live: he had helped her to accept without anxiety whatever their life might entail, whether as workers or as parents. Although their home was unsophisticated to the point of apparent poverty, they had no wish to live elsewhere. They intended, she said, to acquire a second home nearer Chitose, so that their boys would be able to walk to school and back, rather than catch a bus at seven to carry them ten kilometres to their school, with no chance to dawdle on their way home, as children need to do, stopping to look at things in the woods and fields. They themselves planned to come to the farm daily since it was where they worked. As the afternoon went by, I began to feel, as I have rarely felt with anyone else so strongly, that I was in the presence of a person entirely at ease with herself, her presence wonderfully warm and restful, a woman who appeared to wear, as if it were a garment, a habit of serenity.

The dark afternoon was closing in, and it was time for us to be getting back to Chitose. When she had locked the door, Hisako introduced us to the dogs. The sheepdog's name was Indiana; the wolfdog's name was Jones. I put out my hand to touch his head, but he wanted to put his paws on my chest. As they were dark with wet ash, I held them off, gently, so as not to hurt his feelings. Although dogs do not care to be looked at, we regarded each other steadily for a second or two, and I searched for brotherhood in his eyes, one brown, one blue.

We found on returning to the shrine that Toshinori and his friend had placed a couple of spotlights on the grass, their light directed upwards so that the overhanging branches reflected the light back down upon Hisako's woven sculptures, which made them look even more mysterious than before. They lay as if abandoned, vast ultramarine rocks washed up on the beach by an underwater cataclysm, or pieces of a sky-blue meteor that had fallen from space. Mr Matsumoto was going to take us back to the railway station at the air terminal, and as we said our goodbyes to the Sumis, they stood close beside each other and waved, until they merged with the dark background and became invisible. In the days that followed they were planning to build more woven sculptures. As the temperature fell below zero, then much lower, I wondered how they would manage. I am sure, though, that they found a way. The hand of the craft that subdued them and held them in its grip is generous to those who serve it with courage and fidelity, to those who work at their craft with love.

"The dyer's hand" is a phrase from Shakespeare's Sonnet 111, an uneasy poem in which the poet expresses shame that he has to work for his living, and asks his noble friend to pity him for his lowly and unequal condition. Should Shakespeare be speaking in his own person, his shame, so one supposes, would have been the disgrace of having to bear the brand of being an actor, a mere player. Some lines of the sonnet have resisted efforts to interpret them, but lines five to eight are clear enough:

Thence comes it that my name receives a brand,
And almost thence my nature is subdued
To what it works in, like the dyer's hand...

The poet W. H. Auden took the phrase "the dyer's hand" as the title of a collection of essays, mostly about writers, Shakespeare among them. Auden sees the image as a sign of the craftsman's condition, the condition of a practitioner of any craft, not only the writer's craft. It is a condition that the craftsman is bound to accept along with its disfigurements. Indeed, our craft enters into the fabric of our lives so deeply that it colours all that we do as with an ineradicable dye, not only the ways in which we carry out our work, but how we perceive the world around us, and how we perceive our own place in that world. And while the materials and techniques of every trade or craft set limits to what can be done with them, they enable us to work within those limits in order to enjoy the freedoms that they allow us to explore.

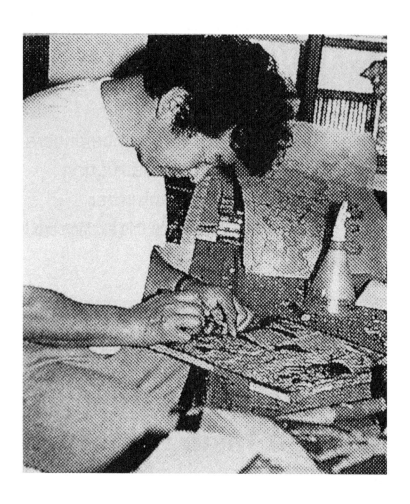

Kunio Sato, wood-engraver

While I was working at Hokkaido University, I used to spend a week in July with graduate students in the Faculty of Fisheries, which has its own marine campus at Hakodate, the city tucked under the heel of Hokkaido's boot. Hakodate is the island's oldest link with mainland Japan and its most distinguished sea-port, architecturally as well as commercially. Where Otaru, to the north-west of Sapporo, is open to trade from Russia, Hakodate faces the sea lanes that lead to the Indian Ocean and beyond, or just around the coast and up the Japan Sea to Vladivostok. When Admiral Perry brought the "black ships" of the US Navy to Japan, this was where they first put down their anchors. I love Hakodate, and have written about it extensively elsewhere.

Mr Urashima was very keen that I should meet Kunio Sato, an engraver who lived there. As Hakodate lies well beyond Mr Urashima's normal beat, he had asked a resident school-teacher, Mrs Shizuko Shimizu, to act as my guide and translator. Two days before we were to meet the craftsman himself – a stranger to us both – Mrs Shimizu came to my hotel, and we sat down to discuss what we might ask him. As Mrs Shimizu did not drive, I supposed that we would take a bus, but since only three buses a day went anywhere near our destination, she had asked a friend of hers to take us by car. The car was antiquated and I had to sit up very straight, my knees high, my elbows in. Just as we were setting off, a downpour crashed down on the roof with a thunder-clap like a sudden Haydn fortissimo. It streamed down the windscreen like a waterfall, as the dark shapes of vehicles whizzed by on either side. The driver behaved towards her vehicle with the casual indifference of long acquaintance; I shut my eyes. "I am doing this for you, Mr Urashima", I said to myself.

Twenty minutes later, alive and unharmed, we reached the house. We were still in suburbia, the houses all relatively new, though the house that we were visiting was older and less obviously designed than its neighbours, and had been built, we were to learn, eight years earlier. It was a small, two-storey house, only a yard or so from the road. The kitchen overlooked a narrow by-road, and a small portico roofed in corrugated plastic shaded the front door. Mrs Sato opened the door as her younger son, fifteen years old or so, fled upstairs. Kunio Sato was sitting cross-legged in front of a low table with his back to the open-ended kitchen. He was dressed in green track-suit pants and a short-sleeved white and yellow cotton shirt; his forearms, the colour of mahogany, were short and rounded with muscle; his hands were square, the fingers huge. His square head was also large, and his round cheeks were as red as fired brick; a heavy crop of black hair, cut straight, fringed the nape of his thick neck. Ms Oido, the etcher, would, I felt sure, have enjoyed drawing a picture of him. The crinkles around his eyes suggested that he smiled often, but, since he knew neither Mrs Shimizu nor myself, politeness dictated that he hung his head a little humbly, not yet quite ready to look at us face-to-face. For all the modesty of his manner, Mr Sato was clearly a man at ease with himself; his wife, a tall and slender woman with a clear complexion and a youthful face, brought us coffee, and though she did not speak, they seemed, across the space between them, to reach out and touch each other.

We had prepared a list of questions, but, perhaps because Mrs Shimizu was a less experienced interviewer than Mr Urashima, Mr Sato's answers did not always correspond to the questions that I thought I had asked, so I hope I have represented what he said correctly. He was born, he told us, in Kitahiyama, a picturesque place, halfway up the shin of Hokkaido's leg, five kilometres from the coast, with woods, rivers and high cliffs that fall abruptly to the sea and protect the town from tsunami that sometimes reach the shore. When he was a boy, he had begun a habit of collecting seashells, which led to his making friends with an archaeologist, a school teacher from Hakodate, who used to visit the area to look for shards of Jomon pottery, and he had invited Kunio-kun to join him.

Now that the boy Kunio has grown up to become Mr Sato, he works as one of a team of carpenters who construct the wooden underframe upon which every Japanese house, modern as well as traditional, is built. His other calling, however, is the engraving of woodblock prints to illustrate the stories of Kenji Miyazawa, a writer of heroic stature for the many who love his work. Some have called Miyazawa the Japanese Shakespeare, though when I asked Professor Watanabe about this, he thought the comparison a little far-fetched. Since every Japanese child reads Miyazawa's stories at school, Kunio had read them, too, or had listened to his teacher read them. At the time they had meant very little, but when he had moved to Tokyo in his early twenties he read the stories again, and had at once felt the powerful tug of home, for he had seen a link between the characters in Miyazawa's Dungari Yama who eat beech nuts, and those who would once have eaten them in Kitahiyama. When the Ainu had lived in Iwate before they were driven across the Tsugaru Straits into the island of Ezo by the Yamato, the forerunners of the Japanese people, they, too, would have eaten beech nuts. When he was a boy Miyazawa's grandmother had told her grandson stories that came out of a comparable oral culture: stories of a boy who takes a train along the Milky Way, of dahlias that talk to each other, of birch trees and foxes who become friends, and of generals who spend thirty years rooted in their saddles. I also knew the stories, because my friend Nobu, the folklorist, had translated them into English, and given me a copy.

Before he told us why he had gone to live in Tokyo, Kunio asked his wife to leave the room as he did not wish to embarrass her by speaking of her in her presence. He had gone to live in Tokyo when he was nineteen because he wished to become a professional painter, he said, and in Kitahiyama he knew he would have had little opportunity to do so. He was unable to realise his dream in Tokyo, but it mattered less, for he had met the woman who would become his wife. They met at a night school while studying Buddhist literature and joined a music club, where he played the mandolin and she sang folksongs. They had married almost at once, and he had had to look for work to support them and their first son, who was born the following year. He found part-time work as a furniture maker, but after five years of little financial success, and now with another child, he decided to return to Hokkaido. When he read Miyazawa's stories again, he felt once more what he had felt as a child, the appeal of the mountains, the pull of the sea, and as his longing to paint them grew stronger, he came back to Kitahiyama.

Soon he moved his family again, this time to Hakodate, not so far away. His father's father had been a fisherman from Kanazawa, and his paternal grandmother had come from farming stock in Tokushima, the prefecture from which many of the original *tonden-hei* had come when transported to Hokkaido by the Meiji government, and where *ai*, the Japanese indigo also comes from. His maternal grandfather had been a wheelwright, and a maker of sledges, and one of his uncles had been a housebuilder. When Kunio was a child he would walk to the village where they lived, to watch them plane planks and chisel joints; he had thought how pleasant and satisfying such work must be. He came to see that working with wood was in his blood, and that the two years he had spent with a master carpenter in Tokyo had not been an accident. In Hakodate he walked the streets until he found a construction company that would give him a job. In the fifteen years since, he had helped to build many houses, among them the one in which we were sitting. And eventually he had realised that although he might have been forced to set his thoughts of painting aside, he could make pictures with the wood that he handled every day. The grain of the wood and the rings of the tree's yearly growth, beautiful in themselves, suggested images that might be released with a little help from a graver's tool. He did not have to go far to find his destiny: it lay there underneath his hand.

Thomas Bewick, the father of English woodblock engraving, and Hokusai, his Japanese contemporary, both used cherry wood, but Kunio preferred the softer wood of the needle-leafed trees to which as a carpenter he had grown accustomed. While many engravers would find the softness of the wood a drawback, for him it was an advantage: the lines of the grain suggested the outlines of the design and were wholly integrated within it; they provided the design's texture, the surface movement of water, the ploughed furrows of a field, the drifting patterns of a cloud, the ribs of a leaf. He had become especially fond of the wood of *matsu*, the pine, though, like Mr Nagao, he also enjoyed working with yew, *onko*. But *onko* has almost disappeared from Hokkaido and fewer engravers than might once have liked to work with it are any longer in a position to do so.

Mr Kunio had come to believe that his life had fallen quite naturally into place, bringing together his interests as a child with his work as an adult, and in tune with the stories of Jomon culture that he had learned from his archaeological friend. His friend had told him that the Jomon people, like the Ainu, had worshipped trees, that Jomon culture, like Ainu culture, was threaded with rivers, rooted in forests. Since the Ainu had woven cloth from the bark of the elm and made clothes from it, Kunio took a fancy to the notion that he, too, might, as well as engraving pictures, also make the paper on which to print them. He visited the prefectures of Fukui and Miyage to learn what he could about the craft of paper production and he experimented with the wood of the mulberry tree, a tree that had been cultivated by the settlers when they attempted to breed silkworms. But he had had no more success with the making of paper than the settlers had had with the breeding of silkworms. The technique was too hard, the tools were too expensive, it took a long time, time that he did not have. He did, though, keep a few samples of his paper-making efforts, which he preserved in a file in his basement workroom, and when later he took us downstairs he would show us the blocks that he was working on.

This seemed the moment to ask if he had sought out anyone to teach him the craft of engraving. No, he was entirely self-taught, and he was still learning. He had, it was true, gone down to Aomori to have a look at the working methods of the engraver Shino Munataka, but he had learned by training his eyes to look, and by plying his hand, by playing with the wood. He had been just as much influenced by painters, and he surprised me by mentioning Constable, Munch, Henri Rousseau and Chagall. Looking at his prints, the only influence I could spot was that of Chagall. He took me up on this quickly: the influence was not, he said, a question of visual style, nor was it a matter of technique; it was the business of the heart, the soul. But he did not elaborate.

Was it possible to make a living as an engraver? No, not really. He still had to work as a carpenter, but as building in Hokkaido is a fair-weather occupation, he was able to spend the snow-sequestered winters at his workbench. When he first began to engrave, he had had to work at night, and he still had to do so if he had a summer commission. Otherwise, he balanced his work between summers as a carpenter and winters as an engraver: as a house-builder out of doors when the sun shone, with his wood blocks in the cellar when it snowed. Kunio was a day-to-day carpenter who built houses for a living, yet had found time to work as an illustrator of books. He was another, like Norio Tokita and Robert Frost, who had had the good fortune to be able to balance his vocation and his avocation.

How had he managed to find a publisher who would take an interest in his work? The answer seemed to lie in the nature of Hakodate itself, for it is a truly ecumenical city. In Japan, many of the ideas and practices of other faiths sit alongside the teachings of Buddha and the animism of Shinto with no sense of incongruity. It is quite common to be married in a Christian ceremony in a room in a hotel designed like a chapel – I have attended such ceremonies – while at the reception the bride will appear both in her European wedding dress and later in a traditional kimono.

Kenji Miyazawa himself was a convert to Buddhism who counted a Catholic priest among his closest friends. In the oldest part of Hakodate, where the isthmus tilts up towards Mount Hakodate, three churches stand at the intersection of four roads, their doors facing each other: Russian Orthodox, Roman Catholic and American Episcopalian.

Kunio's work, he told us, was first seen in public in 1983 during a slide show projected on to the walls of the Episcopalian Church for an audience of children to mark the fiftieth anniversary of Kenji Miyazawa's death. The slides were later shown at the Roman Catholic Church as part of the annual celebration of Tanabata, the night of the star festival on July 7, when according to a Chinese legend, the divided lovers, Vega the Weaver and Altair the Cowhand, are reunited in the Milky Way. On the night of the Tanabata celebrations small paper boats bearing lanterns are placed in a river to float downstream and carry away sins. It is an incident that is echoed in one of Miyazawa's best-known stories, of the boy who dreams that he is travelling with his closest friend in a train along the Milky Way. At the moment when he disappears from the boy's dream, out in the waking world his friend is drowned while setting lanterns afloat upon the water. Later, the boy comes to the river's edge, where his friend's father waits in vain for a sight of his lost son. The river flows on, reflecting the stars of the Milky Way overhead. The dead boy has been absorbed into what Yeats called "the artifice of eternity".

Since many people had liked his slides, Kunio showed his prints at the NHK Gallery in Hakodate and at the city's Hokkaido Shimbun Hall, two places where citizens may, without charge, display their work. A visitor bought a print that he sent on to a friend working at the Hokkaido Shimbun in Sapporo and the newspaper commissioned Kunio to illustrate Miyazawa's story

Serohiki no Goshu (Goshu the Cello Player). The illustrations represent Goshu as a boy, and his house is shown against a background of the moon and the stars, with a watermill, a river, a small train and flowers. A well-known publisher, Fukutake Shoten, then invited Kunio to illustrate four more of Miyazawa's stories as children's picture books in the same large format, and other commissions followed. The illustrations look at times a little like the naive woodcuts in eighteenth-century children's books before Thomas Bewick revolutionised the art of British woodblock engravings. Kunio's designs are bold, the angles awkward and odd, yet the parts fit together in a taut and intricate design that integrates the earth-bound with the stars, the dreaming boy and his dream world. They are bold but tender, and the influence of Chagall may be seen here. But Kunio Sato's real benchmark is the grain of the wood, which provides the texture of the work and unveils its essence: his graver goes with the grain to fashion the swellings of clouds, to follow the ripples of a stream, to eddy with it in the circling of the mill-pool, to trace with it the furrows of a ploughed field. The design raises the grain into prominence, as background or foreground. Nothing quite like it may ever have been done before.

When I asked what happened to the blocks once the prints had been taken, Kunio thought that I was speaking of the prints, which were stored in Asahikawa, which seemed a surprisingly long way away. When he realised what I had been trying to ask, he told us that some of the blocks were kept in the cellar. If he liked the grain, he would use the block more than once; he simply used his plane to shave away the old picture, and this gave him a new block to work with. When I asked how he set about his designs, he said that he waited, just as Mrs Kimura and Mrs Sumi had waited on their looms, for the wood to show him what he could do. He first looked at the grain, and would look at it for a long time. He might make a few initial sketches, but these were rough, since once he set to work the wood guided his tool. I asked if he would show us his graver: it was a narrow, v-shaped blade about one and a half inches long; a small block was attached to its underside and bound to the blade with a strip of leather that was black with sweat. He held the handle of the blade between his thumb and his index finger, letting the handle rest in the groove between them, the knob on the underside resting in the hollow of his palm; he crooked the index finger across the blade. With this simple tool he gouged out the lines. Apart from a pencil and a plane, this was the only tool that he appeared to need. He also kept a few chemicals and some colouring stuffs. I wondered if he wished to extend the scale of the work that he was doing? No, he said. Kenji Miyazawa had written enough stories to keep him busy for years.

He might, in the future, he said, write a few stories of his own: he had some ideas. Then I asked if he felt in any way that he was Miyazawa's reincarnation. At this Kunio's head fell forward in shock. Miyazawa had been a genius, and the idea was appalling. I was shocked too, by my own audacity. I had been asking too many questions. Was there anything that he would like to ask me or anything that he would like to add? Yes, he said, there was. The world was going through a period of unprecedented change and difficulty, and he felt that the stories of Miyazawa had the potential for creating harmony and understanding between races and people and between humans and those with whom we share the world. He wanted the world to know that.

Kunio-san took us down into the basement, where light through a glass garden-door at the top of the steps partly illuminated his work table, a long plank of deal with a stack of prints balanced at one end, while shelves against the wall held reams of paper and piles of blocks, old and new. Among the blocks on the table was one of the first that he engraved, of Goshu playing his cello, a block that he had not cared to plane away, and he showed us how he used his plane, not like a European carpenter who pushes the plane away, but pulling it towards his belly, as if to draw it into himself. As it happened, I had passed a shop in the older part of Hakodate the day before that sold craftwork of assorted kinds, and on show was a piece that the owner of the shop had just brought back from Britain, a toy model of a Welsh carpenter, who, when set in motion, pushed the plane away from his body in the style prevalent in Britain. The owner of the shop was struck by the contrast with the Japanese way. In Japan the belly is the most vulnerable part of the body and also the most valuable, and you draw everything towards it, for nourishment as well as protection.

Kunio showed us a piece of pine, black with ink, pointing out the shaping lines of the grain; he picked up two pieces of wood, not yet used, one a long, narrow piece of *onko*, the other a two-foot-long piece of *hinoki*, white cedar, softer in texture, slightly yellow, eighteen inches at one end, tapering to almost nothing. He spent a good deal of time here, he said, working by the light of a single exposed bulb. Some shelves against the wall at the foot of the stairs held a small collection of Jomon figures and shards of pottery, *objets trouvés* unearthed by Kunio himself while working in the neighbourhood on the foundations of the new houses that seemed to spring up like mushrooms in a damp autumn. Their presence, he said, helped to sustain him in his work.

In the course of my interviews, I had grown attracted to the Japanese concept of *mingei*. The word is translated into English as "folk craft", to distinguish its works from *hijitsu*, fine art, on the one hand, and *kogei*, artisanal objects of utility, on the other. Although the distinction between *mingei* and *kogei* is difficult to draw, what I had understood by *mingei* – and Kunio agreed with me – was the idea of beauty in craftsmanship: that a pot or a bowl made for practical purposes in the kitchen or on the dining table, or a fabric made up into a pair of curtains, can be beautiful, too. A wheel made by his grandfather, to the highest standards, without embellishments and fit for purpose, was no less beautiful, he argued, than the pots made by Shoji Hamada. Since Kunio was a lateral thinker, he followed this comment with the remark that he had once seen a picture of Hamada's face and that it had reminded him of the face of his mother. I thought that Yukio Oido, with her absorption into the characters and faces of her subjects, might have liked that observation.

On the way back to Hakodate, we passed a statue of the poet Takuboku Ishikawa, and paused to have a look at it. Takuboku, as he is universally known, died in 1912 at the age of 26. He lived in Hakodate for just two years, and now, cast in bronze, he sits on a stone plinth facing the sea, not cross-legged but in western style. His right elbow rests on his right knee, his chin rests on his fist; his left hand lies loosely about a book on his left knee. His head is shaven, he looks downwards. His name is embossed on a bronze plate, and a larger plate embossed with a *tanka* sits in the centre of the plinth. Takuboku's *tanka* are forerunners of the kind written by Norio Tokita: they are direct, earthy, outspoken, based upon the real life of ordinary people. Takuboku had no time for high-flown notions of what poetry ought to be, and defended his views, which became increasingly socialist, in a polemic called *Poems to Eat* (1907). Today his poems are known and loved throughout Japan; Professor Watanabe knows hundreds of them by heart. He translated for me the poem inscribed on the plinth, which commemorates the time that Takuboku spent in Hakodate.

the northern beaches
must be smelling of brine
and I suppose
that the sweet briar
will also be again in bloom

Later that spring, I had a letter from Mrs Shimizu to tell me that she had recently been to a concert given at the Satos' house. A Japanese performer who had lived in South America and learned the songs of an Amerindian people, sang to them that evening. In July, I had a letter from Kunio to thank me for the account of our meeting that I had sent him. It is now it is twenty-five years since that meeting, and I have revised the account of it, but my feeling is the same. Kunio's modest success continues. Whether he is still building houses, I do not know.

Makoto Shimazaki, glass-maker

After a slow soak in the hot bath at my Tokachigawa Onsen hotel, I had slept well. At seven-thirty Mr Urashima came to collect me. Although the weather bulletin had forecast rain, a clear sky promised a lovely late autumn day. We set off north across the Tokachi river into suburban Otofuke and passed from one moment through streets lined with blank-faced supermarkets to the next between wide tracts of unhedged fields recently harvested. A solitary windbreak of larch and oaks ran off westward for miles across the fields towards to the wooded foothills of the central Daisetsu-san massif, just then emerging out of the early morning haze. We dropped into a tree-enclosed valley, and after pausing at a viewing spot where Mr Urashima could eat his breakfast, followed a winding gradient down into Ashoro, where, several years earlier, we had come to meet Mr Nagao, the worker in wood.

We passed through Ashoro into the outskirts of the forest that encompasses the Akan National Park and extends eastwards as far as the Okhotsk Sea. Just before we reached the lake-side resort of Akan, where the sacred waters of the lake are encircled by the wooded relics of old volcanoes, we turned north to Bihoro, and not long afterwards arrived at Aioi, a hamlet with a population of 300 souls, where the valley closes in on a scattering of houses; some of them vacant since the railway line that ran down from Bihoro closed ten years earlier. As it was a Sunday and those who worked at the local sawmill were likely to be still in bed, we might have had to wait, but a store was open, and after a few brief words, and with the aid of a map drawn by the man we were to meet, Mr Urashima turned right on to a grass track. It ended in a field of golden-rod from whose dead florets grey seed-tufts were being carried away on the wind. A barn, its vertical cladding painted in creosote that had faded to a dirty brown, its sash windows grey with cobwebs, looked at a distance as if it were embedded amongst the heads of withered flowers.

"That must be the place", said Mr Urashima. He had not led me to expect anything like this, but our jaunts were often, for me, more like mystery tours. In this case I only knew that our destination was the workplace of a glassmaker, Makoto Shimazaki. We were about to run aground in the golden-rod when Mr Urashima turned right again on to a patch of grass in front of a smart, box-shaped dwelling, its clapboard walls newly painted chocolate-brown. A chained dog with the head of a wolf gave warning of our approach, and as we got out of the car our host appeared at the top of the steps to the door. Off we went through the golden-rod and on to the sleepers of an abandoned railway line that led towards the barn, which turned out be an old engine shed where the line from Bihoro had once reached its terminus. The rails disappeared beneath the boarded-up end-wall.

We entered the shed by a small postern in the barricaded doors, from which the track ran on until overwhelmed by a bank of sawdust, piled up high against the wall at the end. A couple of platforms on wheels were still in place on the lines, still in use. Two

kilns, built like pyramids of stepped, white-washed bricks, strad-
dled the lines, their chimneys passing through vents in a pitched
roof braced with beams and strung with cobwebs. We passed
from the engine shed into a small annex with a short passage
that led to two adjacent rooms with windows that looked east to
the wooded flanks of a narrow valley. The rooms had been newly
white-washed, and in one, a store room, shelves were stacked
with plaster casts and plastic cylinders that had been used as
moulds for earlier work, while in the other two bunk beds took
up much of the space. The windows in the passage looked north
and south, and were filled with warm sunlight. Silver birch sap-
lings had grown up against the south-facing wall of the passage,
and on its own platform sat the small mill that Mr Shimazaki
used for grinding glass. Across the aisle, a workbench stood
beneath the north-looking window, a sink alongside; on a chest-
high shelf that projected above the sink a weighty ovoid piece of
moulded glass balanced on the more rounded and broader of its
ends; a surgeon's mask lay beside it on the shelf.

I was ready to learn what to make of these mysterious objects
of no identifiable form. They were not blown like Mr Asahara's
hollow goblets, but baked in a kiln like Mr Sakata's pots, until the
ground glass of which they were composed solidified into a single,
weighty mass. Mr Urashima had told me that Mr Shimazaki
quickly adapted himself to those he was with and his English
turned out to be excellent – he understood what I was asking
before Mr Urashima put my questions to him in Japanese – so
that translation became a distraction. Since his working space
was as clinical as a hospital operating theatre, my first questions
were technical. How did he create these solid bodies of glass?
How long did it take him to make them? Mr Shimazaki asked
us to look at a clay model. Simple though it appeared, he said,

it had taken him two weeks to get that far. When he worked on smaller pieces, he told us, he could make three or four a year, but he preferred to create something that had body, that you could lay your hands on, with reverence.

He showed us plaster casts and a time-chart of the number of days that it had taken him to bake a recent piece of work, once the kiln had been primed with sawdust and he had filled the mould with finely-ground glass. Over the first day, the kiln had been heated to a temperature of 800° Celsius, allowed slowly to fall, with a small peak on the third day, then cooled evenly for four more days, while the molten glass underwent its metamorphosis and became as solid as a lump of rock. If it was a large piece, the cooling might take anything up to four weeks and he would have to check the temperature every two hours, adding sawdust to control the level of the heat, which explained the bunk beds. Still in the engine shed, protected by his mask, he would then grind the surface of the piece and polish it until he was satisfied. As stones and rocks are weathered by wind and rain, so his pieces had to submit to the process of attrition and decay: a piece that had already been displayed was now undergoing further transformation, which might take years. Or a piece might be left to age by itself, which might take forever.

We learned that Mr Shimazaki was not only a modeller in glass, but also a painter, a writer, and a photographer. When he was not at work at his kilns, he paid a weekly visit to an admirer of his work who had bought some of his glass, and for whom he was helping to design a hotel that she was building at Shikaibetsu in the Daisetsu-san National Park. Since he was obviously a man of many talents, I asked what had brought him to seek out so reclusive a place as this. He was not unwilling to tell us. On graduating from Waseda University, he said, he had entered a School of Modern Art in Yokohama, where he studied the theory of art. He had then assisted Nobuo Sekine, a leading Japanese sculptor, who had gone on to become the director of a sculpture centre in Washington, D.C., creating works in plaster, bronze, and stone. Mr Shimazaki, however, had taken himself off to study philosophy in India; on his return, he had lived in the mountains of Kanagawa, where he had helped to build a home at Odawara for the handicapped, and where, he told us, he had learned to make something from nothing.

He had then rented a house near the Yokohama Public Library and devoted himself to a year's reading in science, art history, theology and Chinese poetry. And it was while he was living in Yokohama that a friend told him of a place that might be what he was looking for: Aioi. He was drawn here, he felt, by an invisible thread. The railway authorities had closed the line from Bihoro only the year before he came, which had been nine years before we called on him, and in the engine shed he had found the space that he needed to house the kiln and the larger pieces of equipment that he would require to make his mysterious sculptures; the rooms vacated by the railway workers were his store-rooms. The bricks of the kiln were baked blocks of volcanic ash dug out of the local fields, while sawdust for the kiln came from the sawmill, still in operation, just two hundred yards away.

His impulse, he told us, was not aesthetic but spiritual, and spiritual power was what he wished his works to express. He did not bother whether, in his own or another's eyes, his pieces were things of beauty: working at them was a mode of contemplation in itself, a spiritual exercise. While he was working, he said, he felt himself to be a mote of dust compared with the energies that surrounded him: he was merely a funnel through which all that energy passed. Before he could settle down to his work as a sculptor in glass, he had first to empty himself of daily concerns and close his ears to mundane demands. He had to be pure, as the wind and the water are pure. To this end he engaged in preparatory meditation, which he had learned as an adept of yoga in India, although he now preferred to follow the methods of Shinto and Zen.

I wondered if he wanted those who came in contact with his work to be charged with some of that spiritual energy. In reply, Mr Shimazaki told me of a visit that he had made with friends to the Taj Mahal. The Taj Mahal was far more than a work of physical beauty: they had felt themselves in the presence of a being that had in itself the power to change everything that came within its orbit. So, yes, he said – as if nothing were more natural than that it might be possible – he did wish his pieces to affect those who saw or handled them, to feel what he and his friends had felt on their visit to the Taj Mahal, and he hoped his pieces might charge the air of any space in which they were placed. He hoped that they might be a focus for meditation. Yet for that to happen the observers, too, would have to be in the right frame of mind. They would need to approach the glassworks in a state of emptiness yet be open and ready to respond to whatever the stones of glass might call into being within them.

Where Chiyoji Arashima of Otaru had spoken of his glass as "arrested fire", Mr Shimazaki of Aioi referred to each of his pieces as "awakened stone". He believed that his glass artefacts possessed the same power as rocks, transformed as they were by the same remorseless geological processes. While our first experience of the objects would be visual, he argued, our instinct should be to reach out and touch them – not to own them, but to stroke them tenderly, with untroubled, unpossessive affection. I asked him if he was familiar with the work of Dame Barbara

Hepworth. Yes, of course, he said. So I told him of how, when an exhibition of her work was mounted at the Tate in London the curators had placed ropes around each piece to prevent the visitors from getting too close, Dame Barbara herself had insisted that the ropes should be removed: visitors, she said, had to be able to touch her work, and if as a result some of the surfaces were to wear away, well, that was how it should be. So, with her blessing, I had stroked a column of her work, shaped like a totem pole. It had many facets, all worked to a different finish. The wood under my fingers felt like silk, yet also alive, almost as if it were breathing. Was it something like this that Mr Shimazaki wished us to feel? Yes, he believed that it was exactly that.

We returned to the engine-shed, and through the east-facing windows could see the sawmill. We cast up our eyes to a pulley hitched between the cross-beams. We left the building through the postern by which we had entered, and took a worn pathway through unkempt grass towards a long, single-storey wooden structure, painted chocolate-brown like the house, but less recently. It had been a dormitory for railway workers, but when we stepped inside we found that the walls were white, freshly painted, the floors were carpeted, and that the only piece of furniture in the first of an enfilade of rooms was a beautifully-made modern desk and chair that stood before a linen-screened window.

The inner wall was fitted with a *tokonoma*, the alcove where an *ikebana* display of flowers would normally stand in front of a *sumi-e* ink painting, but the picture in Mr Shinazaki's *tokonoma* was a photograph of his Indian teacher, while on the shelf below stood a record player and a neat row of videos. The teacher's eyes were dark, huge, hypnotic. I shivered slightly. Mr Shimazaki had referred to him as Osho, a name that I had not recognised, but

I recognised the face. It was that of Baghwan Shree Rajneesh, a guru who became famous in the 1970s and 1980s. Two former schoolmaster colleagues of mine had been seduced by the Baghwan, leaving their domestic lives and duties behind in England to follow him to his ashram in India.

We passed along the enfilade – really only a passage – where two of Mr Shimazaki's large and powerful paintings were hanging, to a room at the further end, which was furnished with a square, solidly-built wooden table, and we sat around it on simple chairs. Mr Shimazaki told us that he sculpted with his left hand, but painted with his right, and from a low shelf lifted an oval-shaped stone of glass about nine inches from top to bottom, and placed it on the table for us to contemplate, and handle. It was opaque, dark-green, with touches of rust and black and had been metallised with chrome. It rested comfortably and comfortingly between my hands. Mr Shimazaki said that it contained the power of existence.

This was, he added, a highly controversial view, although perfectly in keeping with Zen Buddhist beliefs about the place of stones in a garden. The head of a Buddhist order, who often visited and stayed with Mr Shimazaki in his northern retreat, had selected one of these awakened stones for his own stone garden. Mr Shimazaki then returned to an earlier theme, which he was anxious that we should fully understand. For the creator of the thing made, he said, the making of it was a method of meditation; to the one who saw it or handled it, it offered a focus for individual meditation. This, if we were attentive enough, would change us, not in terms of anything dogmatic, of a creed, say, that we might believe in, but in terms of our willingness to engage in an act of pure contemplation, of openness to the energy that exists in all of nature's works, even the rocks and stones and trees, in Wordsworth's phrase, that we might, in our ignorance, call inanimate.

On the floor beside the window in his living room, he had placed a lotus-like piece of milky-white glass. I asked Mr Shimakazi how much it weighed.

"Sixty-five kilograms," he said.

"And if it is not too rude a question," I asked, "how much do you yourself weigh?"

"Forty-five kilograms," he said.

Slightly built though he was, I felt sure that he must have weighed a little more than this. I asked him if he could lift it by himself. He said he had worked out a technique. It seemed that the pulley in the engine shed, although heavily festooned with decorative cobwebs, was not just for show, but for moving such heavy pieces.

Mr Urashima began to take photographs. He had been fascinated by a blue bracelet that had been lying on the bench in front of Osho's altar, and that Mr Shimazaki had permitted him to bring along. Now, he cupped it in his hand as if it had magical powers. He asked me to hold it beneath a ray of sun so that he could photograph it as the sunbeam set its blue lights on fire. At this point the peace of the morning was broken by the sudden wail of a mid-day siren. During the week, we learned, it sounded more frequently, but this did not displease Mr Shimakazi: the siren established a rhythm for the whole community, keeping those at home in touch with those at work. Though he worked by himself he did not feel isolated, a sensation that Japanese people do not find it easy to live with.

Mr Shimazaki's companion then brought us lunch: *onigiri* rice balls of brown wild rice, with chopped mountain vegetables wrapped in a fold of seaweed. We ate slowly, slowly drank our cups of tea, and chatted of this and that, of the Buddhist monk with his garden of stones, of the need for outer order as well as inner peace, and the necessity of cleanliness before we settle down to whatever work we have to do. As we made our way out, I noticed on a shelf a round sphere the size of a beach ball, highly polished and as black as basalt. It was just a round stone that one might come across on the seashore, worn smooth by the weather or the waves, but I felt an urgent desire to place my hands upon it. The surface was as soft as a child's hair, and suddenly what lay beneath my hands became a child's head, and I felt a welling up of tenderness. Of all the pieces that we had seen, that was the one that I should like to have been able to place my hands upon every day. It was not for sale, though.

When we returned to the room through which we had come in, Mr Shimazaki went to a cupboard and slid back one of the doors to reveal his collection of books, mostly by Osho, mostly in English. He gestured towards them:

"You may borrow one, if you like.

"Another time, perhaps," I said.

Mr Urashima was intrigued that many of the titles contained the word "love". What did "love" signify in the context of Indian philosophy and of Osho's teaching?

"I think it means this", I said, and gave Osho's sometime pupil, although a man very much slighter than myself, a warm hug.

"That's right, isn't it?"

"Yes!", he said.

Before we set off, Mr Urashima took photographs of the old station to which the villagers would have returned after shopping in Bihoro, uncared-for now and open to the elements. As we drove away into the westering sun, the spires of the tall feather-headed reeds that the Japanese call *suzuki*, a plant that grows on the verges of every country road, were shot through with a brilliant, silvery translucence. Although dark clouds were beginning to gather about the distant peaks, rays of sun broke through them like the blades of an inverted fan and picked out small pockets of upland greenery. The undulations of the lower ranges lay revealed in dark silhouette. The forms of the nearest foothills might have been enlargements of the awakened stones that we had left behind.

Kinjiro Kida, painter

A year or two before he died, my friend Keisuke Kurata, a professor of cultural studies and, like myself, a self-described semiotician, suggested that we take a trip to Iwanai, to have a look at the work of a celebrated local painter, Kinjiro Kida. Iwanai is a small fishing township on the west coast of Hokkaido, just over the water from the Russian port of Vladivostok. It is vulnerable to sea-borne Siberian storms and lies at the centre of a bay whose northern arm embraces Hokkaido's single nuclear power station, though like all Japan's nuclear power stations this was closed down after the Fukushima disaster of 2011, and is unlikely to be back in operation for some time, if ever.

We had lunch at an *o-sushi* bar near the shore, and then crossed the street to the new Kida Museum, a gallery that had been opened the previous year, designed by Kida's eldest son. The museum is a hollow drum on three floors, with rectangular galleries leading off at angles; internal glass walls offer views of a small court, while an observation platform on the roof overlooks the bay and the sheltering cliffs to the north. I presented my *meishi* – the universal business card of Japan – and a copy of

Northern Lights to the young woman at the reception desk, and asked if she could hand them to the curator. As we were making our way around the upper gallery, a young man approached. I recognised him at once: ten years earlier, Atsuke Kume had been a student of mine in the Faculty of Letters at Hokkaido University; he was now the curator of the museum. (Later he would move on to the Sapporo Museum of Modern Art where Mr Naik Satam's mammoth tapestry then hung.) He told us to take our time; he would meet us after we had looked at the pictures. We took our time, then met him in the cafe for a cup of tea. In what follows, I have woven what we saw on the gallery walls with what Mr Kume told us of Kida's work as well as with what I learned from reference books, but most of all with what I read in the English translation of a celebrated novel based on the painter's life, which is where I begin the story.

On a certain day around the turn of the nineteenth century a man walked from his house through an apple orchard. He was haunted by the image of a boy who had recently come to see him. (A century later, I would walk from my apartment to my office over the same ground, but by that time the orchards were remembered only in the names of the suburban streets.) The man was Takeo Arishima, then a university teacher, afterwards to become Hokkaido's most famous writer. In the novel that Arishima wrote about what followed from this meeting, he calls the boy Kimoto. At that time Kimoto was a student at school in Tokyo, where having seen some paintings by the writer exhibited in a Tokyo gallery, he had, while travelling back to his home in Iwanai, sought to meet the writer, hesitating for several days outside the door of his house before he finally found the courage to knock. Although the writer's servant advised his master not to see the caller, he was told to let the boy in. The boy was carrying a bundle of his own paintings, and at first the writer was a little repelled by his manner, a mixture of truculence and self-mockery, but the strength of the paintings impressed him, and the boy proceeded to speak with such a sudden and spontaneous openness, such charming and frank naivety, that he was greatly affected.

Later, on afternoons when the snow came racing in from Siberia, the writer would find himself thinking, as the evenings closed in, of Iwanai and the boy, caught in the path of the storm. Should an acquaintance be going to Iwanai, he would ask for news of Kimoto; but none came. When his wife died, he gave up his university post to live at last as a writer, leaving to agents and tenant farmers the estates that he had inherited near Iwanai around Niseko (small village that is now an international skiing resort). The image of Kimoto had begun to fade. Then, more than ten years after that first brief visit, he received a parcel. At first he thought it contained dried fish: the smell revolted him. He unwrapped layer after layer of oiled paper, as if the layers were, to use his words, the membranes of a lily bud, and inside he found three hand-made sketchbooks of drawings, all in pencil. Had they been plays or poems, he would have been jealous; instead he felt a powerful impulse to see the boy who had drawn them.

Later that evening, the postman brought a letter from Kimoto, explaining that he was now a fisherman living in Iwanai. He had no money to buy the oils with which to paint the mountains in the pencil sketches that he had sent. He wished to paint them so that they would "appear to have swollen up from the ground into the sky". Could the writer tell him if he had any talent? The writer had been hesitating whether to make a visit to his Niseko estates; now he decided to go at once. (What he did not mention in his fictional account, but that his friends later made known when the novel was published and recognised as only thinly disguised fact, was that when Arishima had shown the actual drawings to those friends in Tokyo, they had bought them, and with the money Arishima had purchased oils and brushes and posted them off to the boy.)

The writer sent a letter inviting Kimoto to visit him at his Niseko farm, but when he arrived at the farm neither a letter nor the boy himself was there to await him. He recollected the feelings that the boy had stirred in him when they had met years before, and felt again the powerful link of sympathy he felt drawing them together. A fisherman who longed to be a painter would be undergoing a struggle like his own, he thought, aching to break free of the humdrum concerns of daily life. It grieved him that they had met only for a moment. He longed for a sympathetic companion, and his consciousness of this duality in himself provoked feelings of melancholy. Night fell. He drew down a cotton blind to blank out the snowflakes beating upwards out of the dark night. "You will never come", he said to himself. Just then his farm manager entered the room to say that a visitor had arrived. The writer went quickly to the kitchen. It must be Kimoto, he thought. But here instead was a giant of a man dressed in a dark snow-smothered overcoat. The giant took off his military-style boots and stood there patiently in his bare feet.

"What is your name?" asked the writer

"Kimoto, sir", said the man in the snowy overcoat.

The fisherman's name in real life was Kinjiro Kida, now as well-known in Japan as a painter as Takeo Arishima is well-known as a novelist, and Arishima's story of their subsequent friendship, according to those who have studied the two men's lives, although told as fiction, is substantially true. Arishima's novel is entitled *Umareizuru Nayami*, a book that all Japanese readers know; they know as well that Kimoto is Kida, that the writer is Arishima himself, and that until Arishima's death some years later, his and Kinjiro Kida's lives were to become closely entwined. The English title of the novel, as translated by Seiji Fujita, is *The Agony of Coming into the World*. The agony is the pain of those who must struggle to fulfil their natures, but who through their position in life have no option but to deny their calling.

In the novel, as they talk through the night, Kimoto tells the writer the story of his life since his visit ten years before. He had gone to school in Tokyo because his family had at that time been able to afford it, but mistakes in the building of a breakwater at Iwanai had deprived the harbour of its hoped-for future as a substantial port, and his family of their traditional fishing grounds. He had given up his studies in Tokyo because his family needed his labour, and his sense of duty had been more demanding than his longing to paint. Yet he would still, when spared from his duties at sea, go off with his sketchbook in search of subjects to draw. When he looked at a mountain, he forgot everything else, so that people called him crazy, but he wanted to contemplate the mountains with complete attention, until he and the mountain became one, and then to communicate his sense of that union through the paint to which he felt as irrevocably drawn. "But I haven't done so yet," Kimoto tells the writer.

The following morning, as Arishima tells the story, Kimoto put on his boots and set off, his bare black head growing fainter as the snow swirled around it, not the delicate boy of the writer's memory, but a man toughened by toil, who had grown to be as strong as a tree. Arishima knew that most men are forced to give up the dreams of their youth because of their need to earn their daily rice, but he saw that in spite of having to bend to the discipline of a fisherman's life, Kimoto had remained faithful to the dictates of his heart.

The authors of critical studies, the curators of exhibitions and the compilers of catalogues raisonnés all assume that when Arishima describes watching Kimoto disappearing into the snow, he is speaking *in propria persona*. And as Kimoto's tender heart and manly courage had caused the writer to feel ashamed of his own weakness, so, on the writer's return to Tokyo, the focus shifts. In a passage which suggests that Arishima had made a study of Joseph Conrad and J. M. Synge, he attempts to place himself within the world of the endangered fishermen and the women who wait for the boats to reappear out of the wind-blown snow, so that he might absorb some of the young man's courage and virility. These scenes in Iwanai are based on Arishima's own knowledge of the place, of how, over the course of a day, a mountain will go through many transformations of colour and light, all of which he imagines Kimoto drawing in sketch after self-forgetful sketch.

He writes of the tenderness that he imagines the young fisherman must feel as he watches his father eat a bowl of rice, imagines Kimoto's frustration when he tells his sister to leave her sewing and go to bed so that he can concentrate on his drawings. A woman teases him when – in a pause between the codfish harvest and the arrival of the herring shoals - he goes off to draw a mountain. He calls on his one close friend in Iwanai, a young pharmacist whom Arishima calls 'K', who reads the letters of Michelangelo but knows that he has no choice but to follow his trade, and K's despair infects Kimoto too. All the while Arishima broods on the brevity of life and the hardships faced by the men who must spend wind-swept nights out on the open sea.

Although Kimoto is only happy when he has a pencil in his

hand, he nonetheless still feels guilty when he goes off to sketch, leaving his family to mend the nets and prepare for their next sailing. He frets endlessly, unwilling to accept the fisherman's lot, until at the end of the novel, walking as if in a dream through the dark streets of the town, he comes to the edge of a cliff, where the thoughts of suicide that he has been harbouring begin to harden: "Leap, and all your problems will be solved!"

Of all the details in Arishima's story, say the scholars who have studied Kida's life, this is the one that is false to Kida's character and the known facts of his life. *Umareizuru Nayami* was published in 1918, and Arishima closes the story with the recognition that it is for the young man himself to decide what he has to do, to exist as a fisherman or to subsist as a painter. He prays for his happiness. Yet perhaps he is praying for his own, too. Five years later, at the age of 45, it was Arishima who committed suicide, with a married woman who had become his lover.

A photograph of the young Arishima suggests a British sub-altern in the First World War, with a Wilfred Owen moustache but soulful eyes and a soft upper lip; at the time of his death, he had lost his hair and in profile looks more like a general in the Imperial Army, a change not untypical of the male Japanese face. Kida, on his part, never looks like a fisherman, nor the man one envisages when reading the novel: he looks from the first like a French intellectual, with a skull that reminds one of André Gide, especially when he took to wearing the French beret. (The latter, in the view of the farmer-poet, Norio Tokita, was an affectation, at odds with attachment to a local, rural identity.) After Arishima's death, Kida took charge of his own life as Arishima had done when he gave up his other roles and committed himself to the life of a writer: he committed himself wholly to a life as a painter. It was as if he deliberately chose to take on his friend's mantle, to be the artist that Arishima had willed him to be. And though the following decades were a time of constant struggle and great poverty, he never regretted that he had taken the road less travelled: for him, to live was to paint and to paint was to live.

There is a photograph of Kida and Arishima taken as they walk side by side away from the camera down a dusty road: Arishima, the aristocrat and a childhood playmate of the Emperor Showa, wears a white shirt, riding boots and a white Panama hat; Kida, the fisherman, is hatless, wears a dark kimono, and on his feet Japanese wooden clogs, *geta*. We see that Kida was not the towering physical presence represented in Arishima's novel, and in photographs that were taken of Kida in his sixties, he is no taller than anyone else. It was his moral stature than must have led Arishima to represent him as a giant.

When we walked around the Kida gallery a second time, Mr Kume came with us, and pointed out the first canvas that Kida painted after Arishima's death. Poplars frame a grassy space bounded by shorter trees, beneath a deep blue sky. The framing poplars are a dark green and the upper branches of those on the right are yellow as sunshine floods across the grass from left to right to crumple up against a small blood-red bank. The paint is applied with the tip of a large brush, and neither this nor the sense of enclosure is typical of Kida's later work. What is recognisable is the generosity of the paint and the lushness of the colour. An early painting hints at Kida's later hand: cultivated fields fill the foreground, ricks of white straw in the middle distance; a grove of autumn-tinted trees on a bank toward the right, while on the left we have an unimpeded view of dark blue hills. The paint is applied in horizontal waves, ranging upwards from dark pink, through green, yellow, russet and dark blue; the sky is aquamarine swept with bands of cream. Ten years later,

Kida painted the scene again, and while the colours are more subdued, he had found no need to change his technique: bold, often jagged strokes in bold, leaping lines. The bulk of his work, apart from a few still-lives of succulent and rubicund apples, well-fleshed fish and some rather good portraits, consists of representations of Hokkaido landscapes and seascapes. As Kida rarely travelled, these almost exclusively depict Iwanai and its immediate neighbourhood.

As we walked around the galleries what struck me more and more, apart from the countless pictures of Iwanai's cliffs and its sea coast, was the confidence with which the paint had been applied, the tail of the brushstrokes left jagged like the brush-strokes of an ink painting, as if the pictures had been painted in a hurry. Mr Kume told us that though Kida had studied reproduc-tions and attended exhibitions when he could, he never received any formal instruction, and it is remarkable that from the begin-ning there is no trace of any hesitation in his approach. Even when they may appear a little raw, the paintings are bold, direct, and inherently dramatic. It was surely this abundant, bounding energy that Arishima at once saw and was so moved by.

Many of the paintings are variations on a theme: a steep cliff on the right, in the middle of the canvas the sun about to set in the sea. Mr Kume believed that the work that first shows what Kida was capable of is one of these seascapes, painted on 18 August 1936. A yellow sun sits in a yellow saucer, the yellow zig-zagging down through waves of blue and green, expanding in a halo and spreading on either side like wings; the paint is applied thickly and no attempt has been made to hide the brushstrokes. On the gallery wall beside it hangs another seascape painted sixteen years later: the sun has set, leaving a blood-red smear and some orange ribbons against a grey sky; clouds at the top of the painting are dark blue; a dark blue sea spreads over most of the canvas, spilling in yellow and grey blotches on a shore of dull yellow and green. The cliff on the right, unmistakably the cliff that rises now above the nuclear power station at Tomari, falls to a huddle of rocks washed, or dashed, by the sea; slight variations of profile or of light depict seasonal changes of vegetation; the sea shows many moods, colours alter accordingly; in other scenes, fishing boats in the harbour rock against each other or huddle together; the brushwork is bold and sure of itself.

Where I have used the word "confidence" of Kinjiro Kida, the word that came to Professor Kurata's mind was "courage", for soon after his name began to be recognised, Kida had to face a spectacular setback. Many artists do not really care to part with their work, and Kida did not hold his first exhibition – a thirty-year hoard of paintings exhibited in Sapporo – until 1953. This persuaded the Asahi Shimbun, a national newspaper that supports cultural events, to sponsor an exhibition to be held in Tokyo the following year; but before it could be set up a deadly typhoon roared through Iwanai, and in the fires that followed a thousand of Kida's paintings were lost. As Camille Pissarro had done after the Prussians occupied Paris and burned his work, Kida immediately began to paint again, starting with a picture of the harbour after the typhoon, in blues and blacks, a green sun low in the sky. By 1959, he had painted enough new work for the Asahi Shimbun to stage the delayed Tokyo exhibition, which was followed by another in 1962, the year of his death.

Amongst the several works by Kida that hang in Sapporo's Museum of Modern Art, Professor Kurata liked best the painting where the sun, which as always in Kida's work sits low on the horizon, is depicted as two fuzzy overlapping globes of green, each encircled by a crimson ring, as purple balls seem to shoot outwards and upwards, while the bottom half of the painting is made up of short vertical strokes of green, yellow, russet and black. The painting bursts upon the viewer like a prism exploding, the lines swell and rebound, as Kida himself did after the fire, with a newly-found vigour. While the colours are as ravishing as ever, he had begun to outline features with blacks and greys, sometimes hatchings, sometimes scraping the paint away with a fine point; he had begun to apply the paint with even more bravura, a kind of carefree energy, while all of the paintings are imbued with his lasting love of the natural world, in the wild leaping and falling of the cliffs and the curling onrush of the waves, all balanced in a harmony of colour and line.

Towards the end of *Umareizuru Nayami*, Arishima imagines Kimoto battling with himself over his need to paint and his feeling of guilt that he contributes nothing to the well-being of his community. Posterity, however, has resolved his dilemma: once rejected as an obscure, struggling painter wasting his time, Kida is now Iwanai's most famous son, and Iwanai, like Arishima's old farmhouse at Niseko, is an important station on the tourist trail of western Hokkaido. Professor Kurata and I stayed overnight at the Kogen Hotel a mile or so to the south of the town, on a slight hill at the foot of a ski slope to the south behind it. When I drew back the curtains in the morning, I looked north over a treeless slope, where a group of scattered sculptures was half-hidden by snow. A belt of trees crossed the view; beyond the trees, more snowy fields and bands of darker trees, while further down the hillside the low roofs of Iwanai appeared to have sunk into deep bolsters of eiderdown. It was the first Sunday of the New Year, and the only sign of life was the blinking red light of a stationary police car. I could just make out the white crests of waves rolling into the bay from the left; dark snow clouds sometimes lifted beyond the bay to reveal the steep, ragged cliffs at whose foot lay the nuclear power station, its two shallow domes like gull's eggs in a nest as they merged with the snowy background. The cliffs that rose above it were the same cliffs that Kida had drawn and painted so many times, seen now by me from much the same point on the hillside where he would have sat on the ground to draw them.

The hotel belonged to Toshizo Arai, a Tokyo publisher who seven years before had added a gallery for a collection of Picasso etchings that he had bought from an American collector. His wife had commissioned a number of Japan's leading painters to depict scenes from Arishima's novel, and she had housed their impressive contributions in an extension to the Picasso gallery, which we visited after breakfast on the Sunday morning before we caught the bus back to Sapporo. Before breakfast I had made a sketch from my bedroom window, which Professor Kurata showed to Mr Arai when we met him later. Mr Arai was pleased, for I had drawn a larch that stood in front of my window, its branches lopped, but its spire untrimmed. Everyone had advised him to have the tree chopped down, but he saw it as a symbol of hope and the virtue of persistence.

I did not know then that this account of Takeo Arishima and Kida Kinjiro was to be the last of the essays that I wrote for Mr Urashima. Not long afterwards he decided that the internet might serve his purposes better than an annual printed magazine. So my expedition to Iwanai with Professor Kurata was the final stage in my exploration of the world of the craftsmen and craftswomen who live and work in Hokkaido. Today, over two decades later, most of Hokkaido remains relatively unchanged. It is a land that has, happily, still been hardly touched by industry; its landscapes are striking evidence of how human beings and the natural world can live in fruitful harmony with each other, if, on our part, we have good will and a commitment to work with nature – as the craftsmen and craftswomen of Hokkaido do – rather than using nature for our own self-aggrandisement.

Also published by City of Words

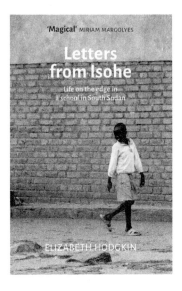

Letters from Isohe
Life on the edge in a school in South Sudan
BY ELIZABETH HODGKIN

After the independence of South Sudan Elizabeth Hodgkin, a historian and human rights researcher, taught in a remote village in the Dongotono Mountains. Her letters home – joyful, comic and terrifying by turns – portray a world where rainmakers, grandmothers, gunmen, teachers and priests strive to live from day to day, and young people yearn for education to guide them in world of danger.

ISBN 978-1-9160783-2-1

Also published by City of Words

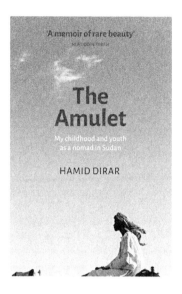

The Amulet
My childhood and youth
as a nomad in Sudan
BY HAMID DIRAR

An intimate account of childhood in a world of sheikhs and
matriarchs, camel-raiders and night-hunters. Hamid Dirar's
memoir ranges from his ancestral homeland in Nubia,
the land of rocks, to the seasonal settlements of the Butana,
the great grass plain. It is a realm of violence and beauty, with
its own laws, where the modern world is a speck
on the horizon.

ISBN 978-1-9160783-1-4

Printed in Great Britain
by Amazon